ORACLE GOD
DEVOTIONAL
JUL-DEC 2024

© Stevie Okauru

ZONAZIN PRESS

NEW YORK   NEW DELHI   TORONTO   SIDNEY

Copyright © 2024 by Stevie Okauru

All rights reserved. No part of this publication may be reproduced, distributed, or transmitted in any form or by any means, including photocopying, recording, or other electronic or mechanical methods, without the prior written permission of the publisher, except in the case of brief quotations embodied in critical reviews and certain other noncommercial uses permitted by copyright law. For permission requests, write to the publisher, addressed "Attention: Permissions Coordinator," at the address below.

Zonazin press
www.zonazin.com

Ordering Information:
Quantity sales. Special discounts are available on quantity purchases by corporations, associations, and others. For details, contact the publisher at the address above.
Orders by U.S. trade bookstores and wholesalers. Please contact Big Distribution:

visit www. oraclemiracle.org.com.

Printed in the United States of America

ORACLE OF GOD
I N T ' L   M I N I S T R I E S

AN INTERNATIONAL FULL GOSPELAND DELIVERANCE PRAYER MINISTRY

Someone once said "They that walk; walks with the multitude. They that run runs with a few and they that fly, fly's alone". And then somebody added "If you want to be among the many, all you need is common sense, you don't have to think before you walk. If you want to run with the few you need advice but if you want to fly you need instruction. That is why those who teach pilots to fly are called flight instructors.

Are you ready to fly? Then be instructed!

Stevie Okauru, the Oracle of God.
Founder & Senior Pastor

ORACLE OF GOD

© Stevie Okauru

ZONAZIN PRESS

NEW YORK   NEW DELHI   TORONTO   SIDNEY

Monday, July 1st

ONE-YEAR BIBLE PLAN: JOB 20-22/ ACTS 11:1-30

Psalm 47:4-7: *"…. Sing praises: sing praises unto our King. For God is the King of all the earth: sing ye praises…"*

PRAISE GOD!

Praise and glorification release the Glory of God and the anointing power of the Holy Spirit into every area of your life. As you sacrificially praise Him, you offer thanksgiving for His mercy, His grace, His goodness, His power, His healing, His love, His favor, and all His blessings. Praise the Lord now! *And the spirit of excellence shall come upon you in Jesus' Name. Amen!*

PRAISE AND WORSHIP GOD NOW!

Bless His Holy name, tell Him, He is worthy to be praised and adored; He is worthy to be magnified. Give Him all the glory, honor, and adoration. He is the King of kings, the Lord of lords, the I am that I am, the ancient of days. He is the only one who can do marvelous things in your life. He is the miracle-working God. He is the only one who can make the impossible possible in Jesus' Name!

BIRTHDAY AND ANNIVERSARY PRAYERS!

Lord, I commit all the July children into your hands; it is the seventh month of the year, the month of perfection; perfect everything that concerns them; from all over the world, and from above, send them blessings. Give them a new beginning of joy, success, and promotion, and help them serve you more this year in Jesus' Name. Amen!

Tuesday, July 2nd

ONE-YEAR BIBLE PLAN: JOB 23-24/ ACTS 12:1-25

Hebrews 3:1: *"Wherefore, holy brethren, partakers of the heavenly calling, consider the Apostle and High Priest of our profession [or confession], Christ Jesus."*

OUR HIGH PRIEST

Few believers today understand the mystery of the apostleship and priesthood of Jesus. Apostle means "sent one." So, Jesus was sent by God to serve as our High Priest. And many don't know what a high priest does. In reality, a high priest is authorized to administer, execute, implement, and carry into effect God's will. **Hebrews 3:1** says that Jesus is the High Priest of our confession. He's sent to put into effect, execute, and carry out our words.

And you've been confessing what you feel instead of Words of faith. If, for example, you're speaking sickness, what will He do with that? He's not a High Priest over sickness. He can't execute that. If you're saying, "I'm so weak, I'm so tired," He can't carry that out. The Bible says, "Let the weak say, I am strong!" When you say you are strong, Jesus can administer strength unto you.

Jesus is not going to administer sickness or disease or poverty or sin. He's defeated all that. He is the High Priest over deliverance, righteousness, and freedom. As you come to Jesus, don't speak words of defeat. Speak words He can implement—words of victory. That's what He's been ordained by God to bring to pass in your life.

Wednesday, July 3rd

ONE-YEAR BIBLE PLAN: JOB 25-26/ ACTS 13:1-25

SUCCESS IN EVANGELISM 6/7

GOD OPENS DOORS FOR WORKERS: The Scriptures often speak of the Lord "opening doors" for His servants who are ready to serve Him. Paul wrote about an "open door" of opportunity that prompted him to remain longer at Ephesus – **1st Corinthians 16:9.**

He even wrote of one occasion with an "open door," but circumstances were such that he did not take advantage of it – **2nd Corinthians 2:12-13.**

From the Lord's remarks to the church in Philadelphia, we learn that the Lord opens doors for those He can use. - **Revelation 3:8.**

Thus, if we desire to be used in God's providence to reach those seeking the truth, we must prepare ourselves to be useful! – **2nd Timothy 2:20-21.**

The principle of preparation applies to both individuals and congregations. Individuals must prepare themselves to teach or to lead souls to those able to teach. Congregations must also be ready to assimilate new converts into the family of God, where they can grow to maturity in their newfound life.

Memory Verse: 2nd Timothy 2:21: *"Therefore if anyone cleanses himself from the latter, he will be a vessel for honor, sanctified and useful for the Master, prepared for every good work."*

Thursday, July 4th

ONE-YEAR BIBLE PLAN: JOB 27-28/ ACTS 13:26-52

Genesis 8:21: *"And the LORD smelled a sweet savor, and the Lord said in his heart, I will not again curse the ground any more for man's sake...."*

KINGDOM COMMITMENT

It is a New Season, so you've got to re-evaluate your commitments. You've got to re-evaluate your giving and tithing. You can't continue the way you've been doing things. You can't do business as usual and claim God's blessings; it will be tantamount to an empty declaration.

How involved are you on the Altar of God? How involved are you in praying, fasting, studying the Word, commitment, fellowship, tithing, and seed faith? Do you want to know how Noah rebuilt with speed? The secret is in **Genesis 8:22.**

There will be no more devastation once you plug into divine principles and wisdom that can never be violated. It would be best for you this year to connect with divine wisdom, and your world will no longer be destroyed. **Genesis 9:1-2.**

God said: Noah, you will produce and not be stranded. Your progress begins with your commitment to God. To succeed, you must prioritize God in every area of your life for the remaining months of this year. Be blessed!

Prayer:

I receive grace for more kingdom commitment.

Friday, July 5th

ONE-YEAR BIBLE PLAN: JOB 29-30/ ACTS 14:1-27

Proverbs 4:18 AMPC: *"But the path of the [uncompromisingly] just and righteous is like the light of dawn, that shines more and more (brighter and clearer) until [it reaches its full strength and glory in] the perfect day…"*

EXTRAORDINARY FUTURE

We all face challenges. We all have obstacles to overcome. But if we can keep the right perspective, it will help us stay in faith to move forward into victory.

You may feel that your challenges are overwhelming, but one thing I've learned is that ordinary people have ordinary challenges. And you're not ordinary. You are extraordinary. God breathed His life into you. And extraordinary people have extraordinary challenges in life.

And the good news is that we serve an exceptional God! When you have an extraordinary problem, be encouraged, knowing that you're an extraordinary person and have an extraordinary future. Your path is shining brighter and brighter because of your extraordinary God! Be encouraged today because your life is on an extraordinary path. Keep standing in faith and declaring God's promises of victory in your life!

Prayer: *Father, I know You have given me an extraordinary future. I stand in faith, knowing You have a wonderful plan for me in Jesus' Name. Amen!*

Saturday, July 6th

ONE-YEAR BIBLE PLAN: JOB 31-32/ ACTS 15:1-20

JULY PRAYER FIRESTORM

Ezra 3:1: *"And when the seventh month had come, and the children of Israel were in the cities, the people gathered together as one man to Jerusalem."*

FIRESTORM DELIVERANCE PRAYER

- *Father, thank you for safely bringing me and my family to the seventh month of this year.*
- *Thank You for bringing to today's prayer firestorm!*
- *Lord, I thank You because You will perfect everything concerning me and my family this month.*
- *Spirit of fear pressing down my inner treasure, I bind and cast you out in the Name of Jesus!*
- *My inner treasure arises and shines this month by fire!*
- *Evil arrows fired into my inner treasure backfire.*
- *Cauldron of imperfection assigned against my perfect testimony this month, break, in Jesus' Name.*
- *Lord! Let my inner treasure arise and shine this month!*
- *Witchcraft spell, upon my inner treasure, perish now.*
- *Rock of Ages! Smash to piece every altar of discouragement in my life in the Name of Jesus!*
- *Stubborn power, behind my stubborn problems, lose your power now.*

- *The evil meeting summoned against me, and my family becomes desolate now in the Name of Jesus.*
- *Troublers of the Israel of this Ministries, the God of Elijah, to trouble you in the Name of Jesus.*
- *Every spirit attacking the commitment and dedication of church members perish now in the Name of Jesus.*
- *O God, arise and scatter every power saying no to the growth of this Ministry in the Name of Jesus.*
- *Lord, uproot every backsliding spirit in this Ministries.*
- *Battles waged against my perfect breakthrough; die in Jesus' Name this month.*
- *The power of inherited frustration in my life perish.*
- *O God, arise! And empower my inner treasure for a perfect breakthrough this month! In Jesus Name.*
- *Ancestral evil that is frustrating my inner treasure; I stop before you stop me in the Name of Jesus!*
- *The evil tongue of discouragement against members of this church, be silenced and condemned forever!*
- *Mouth of evil prophecy assigned to stop the Oracle of God Ministries; we stop you before you stop us!*
- *Let's begin to Thank God for answered prayers.*

First Sunday in July

ONE-YEAR BIBLE PLAN: JOB 33-34/ ACTS 15:21-40

SUCCESS IN EVANGELISM 7/7

GOD OPENS DOORS FOR PREPARED WORKERS:

Many congregations may not find "open doors" to reach others because they have not prepared themselves to be where "babies in Christ" will be cared for properly.

The Lord's providence would never "open doors" for a congregation filled with "Carnal Christians" who would only devour the new converts.

God may wait a long time before providentially working to see that a truth seeker has an opportunity to hear the gospel. Of course, we would anticipate that God would use His providence to spare the truth seeker's life until there are people ready to teach and receive them into the family of God. So, if we prepare ourselves to be useful to God, His providence will "open doors" of opportunity for us to reach those in our community who have honest and good hearts seeking the truth.

PRAYER IS THE CATALYST IN EVANGELISM:

As God's providence works with the lives of those prepared to be used and those seeking the truth, it becomes easy to see how prayer plays an important role.

1. In the case of Cornelius, his prayers prompted God to take notice of his hunger for the truth - **Acts 10:1-4.**

2. He was given to prayer, so God chose to reach him - **Acts 10:9.**

Preparation for evangelism differs from preparing to make a sales pitch. People think that the desired results must necessarily follow if you follow the right procedure with anyone. Certainly, that is not true. Yet prayer is hardly stressed in many books on evangelism. In contrast, we find Paul teaching the Colossians to pray that God would open a door for the Word – **Col. 4:3**.

Prayer is a "catalyst" that starts the process of God's providence in bringing together the lost but seeking soul with the prepared servant of the Lord. When we have prepared ourselves to be useful to the Lord and then diligently pray thus, *"Lord, lead me to some lost soul today,"* doors will open, and we will begin to find souls who have been praying and willing to receive the gospel!

- **Perseverance is the key to success in evangelism;** those who persist in sowing the seed of perseverance eventually bear fruit.
- **The wrong perspectives produce negative attitudes and eventual failure.**
- **The right perspectives maintain positive attitudes and eventual success!**
- **The perspectives we have learned will help us maintain the positive attitude necessary to persevere until Harvest time—1st Cor. 15:58.**

Memory Verse: 1st Corinthians 15:58.

Monday, July 8th

ONE-YEAR BIBLE PLAN: JOB 35-37/ ACTS 16:1-38

2nd Kings 2:1-9 NIV: *"…Yes, I know," Elisha replied, "so be quiet." Then Elijah said to him, "Stay here, Elisha; the LORD has sent me to Jericho."*

BE FOCUSED!

Only focused men and women make it big in life. They are not distracted by sideshows. Elisha was one of such people. As soon as he made up his mind on what he wanted, he refused to accept any other thing short of success. Otherwise, the mockery of the other sons of the prophet was enough discouragement to end his pursuit. His firm resolve was proven by not even Elijah's counsel that he should go back or wait behind could deter him. Instead, he used every discouragement to encourage himself. Surely, such behavior is worth emulating.

Naturally, everyone on a great assignment faces one form of distraction. When it does not come from people around you, it comes from difficult circumstances. Your response to such distractions determines the level of success you attain. If you allow yourself to be weighed down, you eventually lose out on your goal, but if you ignore the distractions, you eventually succeed. Are you facing one form of challenge or the other, causing a great distraction to pursuing your great goal? I admonish you, brethren, stare on straight ahead. Remain focused.

Prayer: *I declare I shall remain focused on my goals!*

Tuesday, July 9th

ONE-YEAR BIBLE PLAN: JOB 38-40/ ACTS 17:1-32

Matthew 16:25: *"For whosoever will save his life shall lose it: and whosoever will lose his life for my sake shall find it."*

LEAVE THE LOW-LIFE

There's the high life or the low life? Divine life or secular life? You can't have them both. It's one or the other. You have to choose. You may try to put off that choice and hang on to the low life while reaching out for the high life to see if it's something you want before you give up everything the world offers. But you're not that tall!

You'll never be able to sample the high life for yourself until you're willing to let go, take God at His Word, and trust Him to care for you. And when you do that? You'll start living the kind of life God describes in **Psalm 1:3.** Your roots will go down so deep that no drought can dry you up, and no storm can blow you down. No matter what happens in the world around you, you'll prosper.

The stronger the wind blows, the more you bend in the breeze. Depression and inflation won't be able to break you. When the rains stop coming, and everyone else is withering away, you'll keep thriving and bearing the fruit of the spirit because you're drawing nourishment from the riverbed! That's what the high life is like, and there's nothing the world has to offer that can even compare. I know that from experience. *Once you dare to let go and trust God, you will testify in the Name of Jesus.*

Wednesday, July 10th

ONE-YEAR BIBLE PLAN: JOB 41-42/ ACTS 18:1-28

EVANGELISM MADE PERSONAL 1/8

The importance of sharing the gospel with others cannot be overemphasized. Jesus wants everyone to hear the Good News of Salvation - **Mark 16:15-16**.

He has provided the gospel as God's power to save all who believe - **Romans 1:16-17**.

But what is the most effective way to reach people today?

What was responsible for your coming to Christ and this church?"

Your answer may include one of these:

- a) I had a special need.
- b) I just walked in.
- c) I liked the minister.
- d) I visited.
- e) I liked the Bible classes.
- f) I attended a revival of the church.
- g) I liked the church programs.
- h) A friend or relative invited me.

What can we learn from all these reasons?

- **a)** It shows different reasons why people join a church or come to church.

b) The preachers must give special regard to the quality of their Sermons and Bible Studies.

c) If churches are to grow, it will be through the efforts of individual members!

d) Preachers, programs, and classes may help, but in most cases, they will only maintain the size of the congregation.

e) Congregational efforts are worthwhile, for they can reach people we might never contact.

f) The greatest potential lies with people who have some contact with local congregation members.

Two things are needed to utilize contacts made through members of the congregation.

a) **Concern for lost souls** by members - **Matthew 9:36-38; Romans 10:1.**

b) **Knowledge of how to increase opportunities to share the gospel:** There are three simple steps to increase opportunities for sharing the gospel with relatives, friends, neighbors, and others. We shall study them in our next lesson.

Memory Verse: Matthew 9:37-38: *"... The harvest truly is plentiful, but the laborers are few. 38 Therefore pray the Lord of the harvest to send laborers into His harvest."*

Thursday, July 11th

ONE-YEAR BIBLE PLAN: PSALM 1-3/ ACTS 19:1-20

1st John 4:8: *"He that loveth not knoweth not God; for God is love."*

THE LOVE OF JESUS

Let's dwell on the enduring promise of **Hebrews 13:8.** In our ever-changing world, this scripture stands as a timeless beacon, assuring us that Jesus Christ remains constant. His character, love, and truth are the same across all ages. C.S. Lewis said, *"Though our feelings come and go, God's love for us does not."*

Jesus, the same figure who walked the roads of Galilee, who spoke Words of life and performed miracles, who suffered, died, and rose again, is with us now. His character, love, and promises remain unaltered through the ages. This enduring constancy of Jesus is our anchor amidst life's storms. The truths He declared, the love He showed, and the salvation He offered are as real and accessible today as they were two thousand years ago.

Today, carry this truth in Your hearts. As you face the ever-shifting tides of life, hold fast to the unchanging nature of Jesus. His steadfast presence offers you peace in chaos, guidance in uncertainty, and hope in despair.

Ask Yourself as you meditate: *How can the unchanging nature of Jesus influence my approach to today's challenges? How does this truth shape my understanding of His presence in my life? Remain* Blessed and highly favored!

Friday, July 12th

ONE-YEAR BIBLE PLAN: PSALM 4-6/ ACTS 19:21-41

Luke 6:38: *"Give, and it shall be given unto you ..."*

WHAT YOU GIVE

Life gives back to you what you give to it. We receive in return what we give to life. Life reflects what you give it. If you are good, people will be good to you, but if you are mean, people will be mean to you, too. A man must surely reap what he sows. **Galatians 6:7–9.**

Now, let me tell you a story: "One day, someone told his neighbor that there was a town where people did not smile at each other. He said, "In this town, everyone frowns at each other. Everyone wears a depressive appearance." His neighbor responded, "Really? Alright! I will go to that town. Please take me there."

So, they went to the town. As soon as they entered the town, the neighbor started smiling and greeting everyone from the entry point. He smiled at everyone he saw. He greeted the people he saw, "Hello! How are you?" with a smile. And everyone he greeted with smiles smiled back at him immediately. He went to that town to confirm if anyone smiled in that town. And he discovered that for every person he smiled at, he received the harvest of smiles on the spot. This is how life should be. *Today, give good and receive in Jesus' Name. Amen!*

Prayer: *I receive the grace to sow positive and quality seeds into people's lives in Jesus' Name. Amen!*

Saturday, July 13th

ONE-YEAR BIBLE PLAN: PSALM 7-9/ ACTS 20:1-19

WISDOM OF THE ORACLE

Isaiah 50:4: *"The Lord God has given Me. The tongue of the learned. That I should know how to speak. A word in season to him who is weary. He awakens Me morning by morning; He awakens My ear to hear as the learned."*

VALUE TO YOUR DAY

- The voice of God you hear in the morning gives value to your day.

- The value of each day is defined by one's heed to God's voice in the morning – **Isaiah 50:4; Psalm 143:8.**

- What you secure in the morning is what he reflects in the daytime.

- Victory or defeat, gain or loss, is not determined at mid-day or later but in the morning, at the onset, not at the end of the day, at sunrise, not sunset.

- Learn to wake up your ears to His wake-up voice.

Second Sunday in July

ONE-YEAR BIBLE PLAN: PSALM 10-12/ ACTS 20:20-38

EVANGELISM MADE PERSONAL 2/8

CREATE A LOVING, EDIFYING CHURCH:

To validate our claim to Christ's disciples. Correct doctrine, worship, etc., are certainly important. God intended to use our love for one another to convince the world that we are His disciples! **John 13:35.**

Our love makes us useful to the Lord: God knows His Churches, and He "opens doors" for those who can be useful to Him—**Revelation 3:7-8.** If we are not a place where new Christians can grow spiritually in an atmosphere of love, God will not use His providence to lead us to souls seeking the truth. Even if we did reach souls for Christ, they would not receive the spiritual nourishment necessary to remain faithful.

Hospitality prepares us for personal work that most effectively leads others to Christ. This is friendship evangelism, also known as relationship or lifestyle evangelism. Which requires a willingness to be hospitable toward those we are trying to reach. We can only practice hospitality towards others if we are willing to practice it towards the brethren. If we will be fruitful in the long run, we must ensure that we provide the right kind of loving and caring environment in the church.

Memory Verse: John 13:35: *"By this, all will know that you are My disciples if you love one another."*

Monday, July 15th

ONE-YEAR BIBLE PLAN: PSALM 13-15/ ACTS 21:1-20

Mark 1:16-20: *".... Come ye after me, and I will make you to become fishers of men...."*

ORDAINED FOR EXALTATION

When Jesus met most of His twelve disciples, they were ordinary men without special attributes. They were largely obscure, uneducated men. But at the end of their lives, they had all become famous men whose lives and activities defined world history. Looking at their backgrounds, there were no spectacular reasons Jesus chose them. If they were the only fishermen in the land, one would have said that was why Jesus chose them. But they were not. Yet He chose them. I believe they were divinely favored for great destinies despite themselves.

I want you to know that after you have done your part as a human being, you still need providence to smile upon you to move you to your successful place. The fishermen were doing their job dutifully on the day Jesus found them. Had they continued on their chosen paths, they would, at best, have become successful businessmen. But that is not the destiny that God planned for them. So, providence made them be at the right place and time. The result was that they were chosen to receive the anointing and grace for ministry firsthand from the Savior of humanity. Are you dutiful in your vocation or profession? *Saint, continue for the day the Lord has ordained for you is coming in Jesus' Name. Amen!*

Tuesday, July 16th

ONE YEAR BIBLE PLAN: PSALM 16-18/ ACTS 21:21-40

John 16:33: *"I have told you these things so that you may have peace in me. In this world, you will have trouble. But take heart! I have overcome the world."*

DIVINE ASSURANCE

Today, be awakened to the divine assurance Christ has given you: In Him, you can find a sanctuary of peace, even amid life's storms. Jesus assures us we will face trials, but He has already written the ending—Victory.

Jesus' Words to His disciples come as both a reality check and a heartwarming reassurance. Yes, we will face difficulties; that's the undeniable truth. But He doesn't stop there. Jesus punctuates His statement with a divine promise: "Take heart! I have overcome the world." These words are our hope amid whatever hardship we are going through. They remind us that we are anchored to One who is greater than anything we will ever face. It's as if Jesus is saying, "Don't just brace for impact; prepare for victory."

Ask Yourself and meditate on: How can you walk boldly today, knowing that Christ has already overcome every challenge you will face?

Prayer: *Lord Jesus, You are my strength, peace, and overcoming power. You've already faced and conquered the world. Help me carry this triumphant spirit into every circumstance today; I pray in Your Victorious Name. Amen!*

Wednesday, July 17th

ONE-YEAR BIBLE PLAN: PSALM 19-21/ ACTS 22:1-30

EVANGELISM MADE PERSONAL 3/8

B. SOME ACTION STEPS TO TAKE:

1. Get to know ALL the members and regular visitors by name. Get a diary and begin to place names with faces. Try to learn someone new at each service.

2. Practice hospitality towards the members and regular visitors – **1st Peter 4:8-9 NIV.**

a. Invite them into your home or out to eat. Try one new family member per month.

b. Visit other Christians weekly, especially the sick, new members, and those absent.

3. Contribute your time, service, and resources to the church. Offer to help however you can: teach, give, serve.

Do not make others beg for help in providing a caring, spiritual environment.

Try to be at every service on time.

When a congregation is filled with loving members who care for and edify its own, it is ready to be used by the Lord to reach out and care for others!

Memory Verse: 1st Peter 4:8-9: *"And above all things have fervent love for one another, for "love will cover a multitude of sins." Be hospitable to one another without grumbling."*

Thursday, July 18th

ONE-YEAR BIBLE PLAN: PSALM 22-24/ ACTS 23:1-17

Matthew 28:19-20: *"Go ye therefore, and teach all nations, baptizing them in the name of the Father, the Son, and the Holy Ghost: Teaching them to observe all things whatsoever I have commanded you..."*

MAKING DISCIPLES

In **Matthew 28:19-20,** The Lord Jesus commanded us to make disciples of all nations. A disciple is someone who follows their leader. So, if someone refuses to "follow" you, you're yet to make that one a disciple truly. The Master's vision is for them to become our disciples, accompanying us and emulating our actions in doing what the Lord asked us to do.

In **1st Corinthians 11:1,** Paul said, *"Be ye followers of me, even as I also am of Christ."* He didn't say, "I've led you to Christ, so follow Him." No! He said, "Follow me as I follow Christ." Thus, when we lead souls to Christ, we must teach them to do what we do and help them cultivate the church habit.

Let them know that church gatherings are mandatory for us as Christians **Luke 4:16.** Don't be satisfied if they only attend special church programs and neglect the actual church services. They must become disciples; for that to happen, we must lead by example. The church is a place of growth, teaching, training, and protection. Everyone needs a family, so bring them into the Church family.

Friday, July 19th

ONE-YEAR BIBLE PLAN: PSALM 25-27/ ACTS 23:18-34

Mark 12:41-42 *"And Jesus sat over against the treasury, and beheld how the people cast money into the treasury: and many rich cast in much. And there came a certain poor widow, and she threw in two mites, which make a farthing."*

YOUR SACRIFICE

In **Mark 12:41-44,** Jesus used this instance to teach His disciples a very important lesson. He did not say these things to this widow personally. God's promises concerning giving assure us that this offering was blessed back to this woman in this life, but the widow did not hear His commendation. There is no indication that this poor widow ever knew that anyone recognized the extent of her sacrifice.

Likewise, sometimes, we may feel that no one knows or appreciates our sacrifices. However, just as surely as Jesus saw this woman's giving and knew of the sacrifice involved, God takes note of our smallest deeds and will reward us one day. God does not judge the size of our gifts by how much we give but rather by how much we have left over after giving. We tend to compare ourselves, but the Lord doesn't judge our giving by what others give. He judges our gifts by what we have to give. The Lord looks at the giver's heart more than the gift. He weighs the giver more than the gift. When we stand before the Lord, all of our works, not only our giving, will be tried to determine what sort – not what size they are.

Saturday, July 20th

ONE YEAR BIBLE PLAN: PSALM 28-30/ ACTS 24:1-27

WISDOM OF THE ORACLE

KEEP TOUCHING LIVES

- Keep touching lives; never care for accolades.
- Never seek for rewards.
- Never be bothered about who appreciates or does not appreciate you or your work.
- Just keep reaching out and touching lives.
- Your reward is sure to come.
- The lives you touch are the ones that will keep spreading the values of your life and ministry.

Third Sunday in July

ONE-YEAR BIBLE PLAN: Psalm 31-33/ Acts 25:1-27

EVANGELISM MADE PERSONAL 4/8

Where does one begin in trying to reach the lost?

II. UTILIZE A PRAYER LIST:

A. WHY THIS IS IMPORTANT: It is a technique used by successful people from all walks of life who have a "things to do" list. It helps focus our attention on those we hope to reach and not neglect them. **1st Cor. 3:6-7.**

B. IN MAKING THE LIST: Start with those close to you and work outwardly: **a. Family, friends, b. Neighbors, coworkers, c. Relatives of fellow church members, d. Regular visitors to church services, e. Casual acquaintances, e.g., mailman, store clerk, etc.**

Limit this list to five or eight at a time. If it is too many, you cannot focus your efforts.

Give priority to the "unchurched" who are not active members of any denomination or church. Active members of a denomination or religion are often very satisfied with their human traditions and are not as receptive to Christ's pure and simple gospel.

Husbands and wives should have one list. Keep this list where you will see it daily.

Memory Verse: 1st Corinthians 3:6: *"I planted, Apollos watered, but God gave the increase."*

Monday, July 22nd

ONE YEAR BIBLE PLAN: PSALM 34-36/ ACTS 26:1-16

Isaiah 60:1-3 ASV: *"Arise, shine; for thy light has come, and the glory of Jehovah is raised upon thee...."*

This passage is written for you. It says you should rise and shine because your light is come, and the glory of God is risen upon you.

But WHAT DOES IT MEAN TO SHINE? To shine is to do something excellently well. When a student shone in the exam, he passed excellently well. When a footballer is shining, it means he is playing excellently well. In **Daniel 6:1-3** Daniel shone among so many others because an excellent spirit was found in him. *And I decree from now, you will begin to excel in the Name of Jesus Christ. Amen!!*

To shine also means to succeed glaringly in a way that cannot be hidden. The day David cut off Goliath's head, he began to shine in Israel. When Elijah called down fire from heaven, there was no doubt any longer who is the Prophet in the land! Your success will no longer be hidden in that Name above every other Name.

To shine is to succeed glaringly and overflow, which means overflowing blessings. Isaac overflowed in the land of the Philistine. He shone when the darkness of famine covered the land; he prospered so much that a whole nation noticed it, and they began to ask, "Why is your case different from ours?" *I prophesy; very soon, people will begin to ask, are you the only one serving God?*

Tuesday, July 23rd

ONE-YEAR BIBLE PLAN: PSALM 37-39/ ACTS 26:17-32

Micah 7:8: *"Do not gloat over me, my enemy! Though I have fallen, I will rise. Though I sit in darkness, the Lord will be my light."*

NOT DEFEATED

Micah 7:8 isn't just about overcoming obstacles; it's a testament to the enduring strength found in God's presence. It speaks to us about the resilience of the believers' spirit when anchored on faith. We are not defeated even when we stumble or find ourselves in moments of darkness. Prophet Micah encourages us to rise, not by our strength, but by the power of the Lord, who is our light. This promise is a beacon of hope, reminding us that our challenges are not endpoints but turning points. God uses these moments to shape us, strengthen us, and demonstrate His faithfulness.

This verse reassures us that we are never alone in uncertain and difficult times. The darkness we experience is not the absence of God but an opportunity for His light to shine brighter in our lives. So, embrace this day with the confidence that God is with you, turning your setbacks into comebacks and your trials into testimonies. C.S. Lewis said, *"Extraordinary hardships often prepare ordinary people for an extraordinary destiny."*

Prayer: *O God, show Your power in my life as a testament to Your ability to turn trials into triumphs in Jesus' Name.*

Wednesday, July 24th

ONE-YEAR BIBLE PLAN: PSALM 40-42/ ACTS 27:1-17

EVANGELISM MADE PERSONAL 5/8

C. PRAY FOR THOSE ON YOUR LIST DAILY: The importance of such prayers is because it is God who gives the increase when it comes to evangelism – **1st Corinthians 3:6-7.**

We are but servants whom God can use in His providential workings. So, though we may work as though it all depends upon us, let us pray as though it all depends upon God! **1st Corinthians 3:5.**

WHAT TO PRAY FOR?

1. The Lord will work with us and give us opportunities to do good for the New Coverts – **Colossians 4:3.**

2. God will give us the wisdom to make the most of those opportunities - **Colossians 4:4-6.**

3. The Lord will give us boldness to say what needs to be said - **Ephesians 6:18-20.**

4. Those on our list will have the opportunity to hear the truth and Have honest hearts to be open and receptive to the truth.

> **Memory Verse: Colossians 4:5-6** *"Walk in wisdom toward those outside, redeeming the time. 6 Let your speech always be with grace, seasoned with salt, so you may know how to answer each one."*

Thursday, July 25th

ONE-YEAR BIBLE PLAN: PSALM 43-45/ ACTS 27:18-44

Matthew 24:14 TLB: *"And the Good News about the Kingdom will be preached throughout the world...."*

PREACH

We are stewards of the Gospel. The power to proclaim the greatest news in heaven or on earth was not given to the angels. It was given to redeemed men and women. Some think that only ministers are to preach, but that is wrong. Every Christian is to be a witness; every follower of Christ is to preach the Gospel.

We can preach by sharing our experiences with others. We can preach by exalting Christ in our daily lives. Sermons that are seen are often more effective than those which are heard. The truth is the best sermons are both heard and seen. They are audiovisual testimony. We can also preach by giving financially to others so they may preach.

Missionary gifts, church offerings, and charitable contributions express your unselfishness and Christian generosity. In all these things, we are partners with God. We are helping by His grace to redeem the world. God's work needs more time, talents, witnessing, and money. Become a full, working partner with God.

Prayer: *Wherever I go today, make me conscious of the people I meet. So, I can speak of You to them, say a kind word, or minister in any way, in Jesus' Name. Amen!*

Friday, July 26th

ONE-YEAR BIBLE PLAN: PSALM 46-48/ ACTS 28:1-15

Ephesians 1:22-23 *"And hath put all things under his feet, and gave Him to be the head over all things to the church, Which is his body, the fulness of Him that filleth all in all."*

CHRIST' CHURCH

Christ and the Church are one. He is the head, and we, His body. In **Acts 9:3-5**, we see the union of Christ and the Church in the dialogue between the Lord and Saul. Before this conversion, Paul wreaked havoc in the early Church and persecuted Christians everywhere until he encountered the Lord, who intercepted him and asked, *"...Saul, Saul, why persecutest thou me."* **Acts 9:4.** The Lord intimately identifies Himself with the Church. An offense against the Church is committed against Jesus. The Lord takes it personally because we're of the same stock.

He's the Vine, and we—the Church—are the branches. He's the head of the Church: **John 15:1-3; Col. 1:18.** The head and the body have the same name, authority, and identity; together, we're called Christ! We've been baptized into the body of Christ. **1st Cor. 12:27; 1st Cor. 12:13.**

The Church, which is the body, doesn't answer a name different from that of the head. So, you're one with Christ. When He was raised from the dead, you were raised together with Him. Now that He's seated on the throne, you're seated with Him in the place of dominion, glory, and authority!

Saturday, July 27th

ONE-YEAR BIBLE PLAN: PSALM 49-51/ ACTS 28:16-31

WISDOM OF THE ORACLE

QUALITIES OF DREAM MAKERS 1/2

I want to share a powerful thought with you today. It will likely turn your life around. It will motivate you to succeed in reaching your dreams and goals. If you can get this revelation in your spirit, you will start down the path of success you have long desired to achieve.

Did you know...?

- o Your decisions have decided your life. God has not decided your life—the moment you accept that, your life changes.
- o God wants you to discover the vivid, definable picture of your future.
- o He wants you to pursue your goals...to reach that future you have been dreaming of—that Dream He has put in your heart and equipped you for.
- o He has given you the special skills, gifts, and abilities...a uniqueness only yours, enabling you to reach that Dream.
- o He desires to have you experience the wonderful reward of success.
- o Your success pleases God. **Revelation 4**

Fourth Sunday in July

ONE-YEAR BIBLE PLAN: PSALM 52-54/ ROMANS 1:1-16

EVANGELISM MADE PERSONAL 6/8

The third step is:

III. INVITE THEM TO SERVICES

A. When you invite new converts, they can see a caring congregation in action. They can see our demonstration of love as individuals, and a church makes a lasting impression! They will more likely have an opportunity to be presented with the gospel. If they attend regularly before conversion to Christ, they will more likely continue to attend after conversion.

B. IN INVITING PEOPLE TO SERVICES: First, pray, asking God for wisdom to invite them in the best manner. And pray, asking God to invite people to attend church service boldly. **Ephesians 6:18-20.**

People will more likely accept your invitations If they are among the unchurched, dissatisfied with where they are attending, and willing to try a different church. And if you have already been hospitable to them severally.

Be persistent: Invite people time and again. Your perseverance will more likely be rewarded if you continue to invite them.

Memory Verse: Ephesians 6:18-20: *"Pray always with all prayer and supplication in the Spirit, being watchful to this end with all perseverance and supplication for all the saints."*

Monday, July 29th

ONE-YEAR BIBLE PLAN: PSALM 55-57/ ROMANS 1:17-32

Job 42:10-11: *"And the LORD turned the captivity of Job when he prayed for his friends: also, the LORD gave Job twice as much as he had before."*

Before God allowed the devil to afflict Job, Job was a man of great wealth. So great was his substance of wealth that it exerted a pull of envy of everyone in the land, even Satan. And the affliction caused him to lose all he had- health, wealth, children, power, everything. The misfortune is enough for anyone to lose faith in God. But Job held on to God. Not even his wife and friends' caricaturing could make him stop trusting God. He kept waiting for a better day, and the day came as God eventually rewarded Him double for all his trouble.

Have you lost all that you had? Are you a shadow of what you used to be or ought to be? Have you become a subject of ridicule because of your afflictions? I admonish you to keep the faith and trust the Lord, for better days are coming. Change is coming for you. Have hope, for hope is essential in the miracle process. Until you lose hope, Satan cannot triumph over you. Had Job lost hope, His story would have been entirely different. But as he kept hoping and trusting the Lord, God moved on his behalf. The God of Job will also move on your behalf as you faithfully hope and trust in Him. He will turn your captivity around for good. *Just have a rekindled hope in God, for this is your season of reparation in Jesus' Name. Amen!*

Tuesday, July 30th

ONE-YEAR BIBLE PLAN: PSALM 58-60/ ROMANS 2:1-15

Hebrews 12:2: *"Fixing our eyes on Jesus, the pioneer and perfecter of faith. For the joy set before him, he endured the cross, scorning its shame...."*

Corrie Ten Boom said, *"Faith sees the invisible, believes the unbelievable, and receives the impossible."* Fatigue can set in in life's races and trials, clouds can gather, and the path can become blurry. That's why **Hebrews 12** guides our focus back to Jesus. Jesus ran His race with a joy-infused resolve, ignoring the shame of the cross for a greater reward: our redemption and His glorification.

With each challenge, recall that Jesus also faced incredible obstacles, yet He triumphed. Because He knew the joy that awaited Him was far greater than any suffering. You, too, can face your struggles, fears, and uncertainties, fully aware that your trials are nothing compared to the eternal joy Jesus has secured for you. So, as you go about your day, recalibrate your focus on Jesus, letting His example of steadfast faith inspire you to persevere and conquer, regardless of the challenges that come your way. What is it that's been weighing on you lately? Just focus on Jesus; He will infuse your day with renewed purpose and strength.

Prayer: *Lord, I fix my eyes solely on You—the true example of unwavering faith and unconditional love. Strengthen me, Lord, to face today's challenges with courage in Jesus' Name.*

Wednesday, July 31st

ONE-YEAR BIBLE PLAN: PSALM 61-63/ ROMANS 2:16-29

EVANGELISM MADE PERSONAL 7/8

C. BE HOSPITABLE TO VISITORS:

Why this is important: By their presence, people are expressing an interest and willingness to learn. By your love and acceptance, you are preparing the soil of their hearts for the seed of the gospel. And because the Lord has provided "an open door," dare we not take it?

How to show hospitality toward visitors: Be friendly to all, whether invited by you, someone else, or simply walk-ins. **Hebrews 10:24-25.**

Arrive early for services: Visitors are more likely to arrive early and leave early; if you come in late, you may not have an opportunity to get acquainted with them.

Give priority to visiting guests over chatting with brethren: You can always visit with brethren later. This may be the only opportunity to make an impact on them.

In extending hospitality, do what is within your ability: Greet them, letting them know they are welcome. Invite them home or out for dinner or a snack. Call, text, write, or visit them after they have attended the services.

Memory Verse: Hebrews 10:24-25: *"And let us consider one another to stir up love and good works, not forsaking the assembling of ourselves together, as is the manner of some, but exhorting one another, and so much the more as you see the Day approaching."*

Thursday, August 1st

ONE-YEAR BIBLE PLAN: PSALM 64-66/ ROMANS 3:1-16

Psalm 57:7: *"My heart is fixed, O God, my heart is fixed: I will sing and give praise."*

GOD MAKES YOU GREAT!

A long time ago, a young man was hated by his brothers, ignored by his parents, with no hope in the world ever to become great. But one day, despite all he was going through, he said, "My heart is fixed within me; I will praise God!" And God said, "Son, my heart is also fixed within me; I will make you great."

That man was David. This month, like David, you can say, my heart is fixed within me; I will praise the Lord. And God will make you exceedingly great.

PRAISE GOD NOW!

Lord, my heart is fixed within me! I will praise you! I will magnify Your Holy Name! I will adore You all the days of my life! I will do Your Will! I will adore You! It does not matter what is happening to me; my heart is fixed. I will praise You! I will love You! I will lift You high daily!

BIRTHDAY PRAYERS:

Lord, thank you for your children born this month. They are children of a new beginning; begin a new thing in their lives, bless and prosper them anew; let it be well with them as they serve you!

Friday, August 2nd

ONE-YEAR BIBLE PLAN: PSALM 67-69/ ROMANS 3:17-31

Psalm 127:1: *"Except the Lord build the house, they labor in vain that build it."*

GOD'S WILL

We are living in a time of monumental decisions and changes. If there ever was a time when we must know God's will and purpose for our lives, it's now. God is rearranging things, lining them up for the end-time move of the Spirit. If you're going to keep up, you must know God's perfect plan for your life—and how to carry it out in His power!

How do you do that? Prayer! God has provided us with prayer in His Word that we can use to receive the wisdom and understanding we need for this critical time we live in. You'll find it in **Colossians 1:9-11.** It's a powerful, Holy Ghost-inspired prayer that will enable you to know God's will and have the wisdom and understanding to carry it out.

That's where most failure comes in Christian endeavors. We glimpse God's will for our lives in the spirit, but then we mess things up by trying to carry it out in the flesh. Instead of letting the Lord build the house in His power, we try to build it ourselves and do it all in vain. Don't make that mistake this month. Instead, pray this prayer that God has given us. **Colossians 1:9-11** is for you to pray. Please put your name on it as you pray it. It's a prayer you can be sure God will answer. Put it to work daily, and God will fill you with His knowledge and understanding!

Prayer: *Holy Spirit, fill me with Your Knowledge and understanding in Jesus' Name. Amen!*

Saturday, August 3rd

ONE-YEAR BIBLE PLAN: PSALM 70-72/ ROMANS 4:1-13

AUGUST PRAYER FIRESTORM

Haggai 2:20-21: *"And again the word of the Lord came to Haggai on the twenty-fourth day of the month, saying, "Speak to Zerubbabel, governor of Judah, saying: 'I will shake heaven and earth."*

FIRESTORM DELIVERANCE PRAYER

- *Lord, we thank You for bringing us safely to August.*
- *I take authority over this month in the name of Jesus.*
- *I will rejoice and be glad this month in Jesus' Name.*
- *I cover every day of this month with the Blood of Jesus.*
- *All things shall work together for good for me this month.*
- *My blessing of this month; I possess you by fire.*
- *The crisis assigned against me and my family this month shall backfire in the name of Jesus.*
- *Demons of get and lose assigned against my home this month, be crushed in the Name of Jesus Christ.*
- *August is the month of a new beginning, Lord; arise and do something new in my life this month in Jesus' Name.*
- *I set ablaze every satanic load upon me this month.*
- *Evil altars set up to make me cry this month catch fire.*

- Enemies waiting earnestly to laugh at me in this month, be confounded.
- Powers speaking sickness and infirmities into my destiny, die by fire.
- Powers speaking sickness and infirmities into my destiny, die by fire.
- According to Your word, Father, keep and shield my family and me from evil this month in Jesus' Name.
- Heavenly Father, help me to continually dwell in Your secret place so that I may constantly abide under the shadow of Your protection, in Jesus' Name.
- Lord, deliver me from the yoke of poverty and burden of infirmity.
- Lord, protect me and my loved ones wherever we go this month.
- Father, open windows of marvelous opportunities for me this month.
- Father, please direct my footsteps and take me to a place of prosperity.
- Come to my rescue, O God, and recover all my stolen favor.
- Lord, remove every evil person around me this month.

- *Lord, cancel every bad vision and revelation upon my life; shan't come to pass in my life in Jesus' Name.*

- *Father, continually renew the strength of Apostle Stevie Okauru.*

- *Thank God for the prayer answered!*

First Sunday in August

ONE-YEAR BIBLE PLAN: PSALM 73-75/ ROMANS 4:14-25

EVANGELISM MADE PERSONAL 8/8

D. MAKE SURE THEY ARE EXPOSED TO THE GOSPEL:

Why this is important: Only the Gospel has God's power to save - **Romans 1:16 TLB:**

Presenting the gospel of Christ: While love and hospitality may help prepare the soil, the seed must still be sown. Ideally, this will come after witnessing a demonstration of the gospel in our lives. By our love, hospitality, etc. Both as individuals and as a congregation

If you feel confident discussing it with them, approach them and suggest some Bible study. If you don't feel confident approaching them with the Word, there is still much good that you can do:

Please bring it to the attention of members and ministers who are able and willing to teach them. Create opportunities for teachers and prospects to become better acquainted; the teacher or minister can take it from there.

You can also encourage them to attend Bible Study and Sunday School, where they can freely ask questions.

These suggestions are offered with a firm conviction that if they are carried out, opportunities to share the gospel and save souls will greatly increase!

With the hope that you will accept the challenge to implement these suggestions. This approach is the most successful in saving and keeping souls and one of the most natural and easiest ways to reach the lost for Christ.

1. Remember, one does not even have to be able to teach to lead others to Christ effectively. One only needs to be a friend to the lost and unchurch Christians to bring them to God's family!

2. Even if we do not convert a single soul, we will have fulfilled our obligation to share Christ with others. We will have done it in such a way as to become better Christians, a better congregation. Better friends, better neighbors, better coworkers!

Are you doing what you can to reach out to the lost?

Memory Verse: Romans 1:16: *"For I am not ashamed of the gospel of Christ: for it is the power of God unto salvation to every one that believeth; to the Jew first, and also to the Greek."*

Monday, August 5th

ONE-YEAR BIBLE PLAN: PSALM 76-78/ ROMANS 5:1-21

Job 22:27-29: *"Thou shalt also decree a thing, and it shall be established unto thee ......"*

DECREE THESE CONFESSIONS

I command every red and white cell to destroy every disease, germ, virus, or alien cell that tries to inhabit my body. In Jesus' Name, I command every cell of my body to be normal; I forbid any malfunction in my body cells. **Romans 5:17.**

For if death reigned by one man's offense; much more they which receive abundance of grace and the gift of righteousness shall reign in life by one, Jesus Christ. The law of the Spirit of Life in Christ Jesus has made me free from the law of sin and death. I refuse to allow sin, sickness, or death to lord it over me. **Romans 8:2.** For the law of the Spirit of life in Christ Jesus hath made me free from the law of sin and death. **Romans 6:13-14.**

Neither yield ye your members as instruments of unrighteousness unto sin; but yield yourselves unto God, those that are alive from the dead, and your members as instruments of righteousness unto God. For sin shall not have dominion over you: for ye are not under the law, but under grace.

Lord, I serve You, and You bless my food and water and have taken sickness out of me. Therefore, I will fulfill the number of my days in health. **Exodus 23:25-26.** And ye shall serve the Lord your God, and he shall bless thy bread and water, and I will take sickness away from the midst of thee. Nothing shall cast their young, nor be barren, in thy land: the number of days I will fulfill.

In Jesus' Gracious Name, I declare. Amen!

Tuesday, August 6th

ONE-YEAR BIBLE PLAN: PSALM 79-81/ ROMANS 6:1-23

Mark 11:24: *"Therefore, I tell you, whatever you ask for in prayer, believe that you have received it, and it will be yours."*

FAITH AND ANTICIPATION

Begin your day with a heart full of anticipation, knowing your prayers are heard and answered. Let your faith be the light piercing the darkness in a world where hope seems dim.

When Jesus spoke these words in **Mark 11:24,** He wasn't giving us a magic formula but imparting a spiritual principle rooted in faith. The heart that genuinely trusts in God's will is the same one that experiences His miraculous touch. This is more than wishful thinking; it's a deep, transformative faith that places absolute trust in God's perfect timing and plan.

Meditate on this: Do your prayers carry a sense of expectancy? Are you ready to receive God's answers, however, they may come? Ask yourself how you can cultivate a heart that trusts God deeply.

Prayer:

Heavenly Father, Teach me to approach Your throne with boldness and confidence. Let my prayers be filled with faith, not doubt, knowing that You are a God who delights in fulfilling Your promises. Help me to trust not only in Your ability but also in Your timing. In Jesus' Name, Amen.

Wednesday, August 7th

ONE-YEAR BIBLE PLAN: PSALM 82-84/ ROMANS 7:1-25

CONGREGATIONAL EVANGELISM 2/3

WHAT IS CONGREGATIONAL EVANGELISM?

A. UTILIZING A CONGREGATION'S MEMBERS:

1. Using the members' contacts: Each member has a network of potential contacts. These contacts may be family, friends, neighbors, or coworkers.

2. Using the members' abilities: Each member has some ability to offer. These abilities may vary, i.e., hospitality, teaching, etc. With any congregation of Christians, there is the potential for evangelism.

B. UTILIZING A CONGREGATION'S ASSEMBLIES:

1. Using the congregation's assemblies: Christians assemble regularly for worship and Bible Study. These assemblies involve worship, prayer, praise to God, and interaction with those present.

2. What happens can impact those who visit: Consider Paul's comments in **1st Corinthians 14:23-25.**

Note that the impact can be either negative or positive. When assemblies are utilized positively, you have "Congregational Evangelism"!

"Congregational Evangelism" occurs when the members utilize their contacts and abilities with their assemblies to produce a positive effect among those who visit.

Now let's consider:

HOW CONGREGATIONAL EVANGELISM WORKS:

A. BY ACTIVATING THE CONGREGATION'S MEMBERS:

I. The members must commit to evangelism – **1st Peter 2:9-10.**

II. The members must invite people to services via cards, phone, and mail or Letters **John 1:46.**

III. The members must extend kindness to those who visit – **Hebrews 13:2.**

IV. The members must display a positive image for visitors - **1st Corinthians 14:23-25.**

V. The members must create teaching opportunities - **Acts 10:24.**

One can learn what to teach.

They can connect the visitor or prospect with a teacher.

Everyone must be committed and do that which provides opportunities for those willing and able to teach.

Memory Verse: Hebrews 13:2: *"Be not forgetful to entertain strangers: for thereby some have entertained angels unawares."*

Thursday, August 8th

ONE-YEAR BIBLE PLAN: PSALM 85-87/ ROMANS 8:1-20

Proverbs 22:3: *"A prudent man foresees evil and hides himself, but the simple pass on and are punished."*

BE PROACTIVE 1/2

Being proactive is being anticipatory. It is change-oriented and self-initiated behavior. It involves acting before a future situation rather than just reacting after the fact. It is taking control and making things happen rather than just adjusting to a situation or waiting for something to happen.

A proactive person prepares to deal with an expected or even unexpected challenge. If you are proactive, you make things happen instead of waiting for them to happen to you. Being proactive is the first of the seven habits of highly effective people.

Proactive people tend to be positive due to the precautionary steps that they've taken for potential "situations." They have more control over their future. A proactive person acts in advance to deal with an expected difficulty.

A proactive choice is based on values and principles, but a reactive person chooses primarily based on desires, feelings, circumstances, conditions, and the environment.

Be proactive and see God change your life and situation for good in the Name of Jesus Christ. Amen!

Prayer: *"Father, grant me the grace to be proactive and not just reactive in the Name of Jesus Christ. Amen!*

Friday, August 9th

ONE-YEAR BIBLE PLAN: PSALM 88-90/ ROMANS 8:21-39

Proverbs 22:3: *"A prudent man foresees evil and hides himself, but the simple pass on and are punished."*

BE PROACTIVE 2/2
TRAITS OF EFFECTIVE PEOPLE

1. Be solution-focused: One of the greatest traits of effective people is good problem-solving skills. We are all going to run into problems sooner or later. It's how you handle them that makes you effective. The most effective way to handle a problem is to focus on finding a solution.

2. Be accountable and consistent:

3. Surround yourself with driven, effective people:

4. Be completely honest about what is not working instead of making excuses. It is easy to stay busy and tell yourself you are taking the right steps, but at the end of the day, you are only doing a disservice to yourself.

5. Consider your options: Being proactive takes time since you must consider your options, weigh alternatives, and make your own decisions to achieve your goals. Don't approach life's challenges by being reactive. Be proactive.

6. Prepare for the possibilities before they arrive. Aim at identification and exploitation of opportunities and in taking preemptory action against potential problems and threats instead of solving a problem after it occurs.

Prayer: *"Father, grant me the grace to imbibe the effective traits in the Name of Jesus Christ. Amen!*

Saturday, August 10th

ONE-YEAR BIBLE PLAN: PSALM 91-93/ ROMANS 9:1-16

WISDOM OF THE ORACLE

QUALITIES OF DREAM MAKERS 2/2

- God's Law is designed to work with great thinkers.
- Great thinkers have "Empires" in their Minds.
- It would be best to have some Empires in your Mind to have an uncommon, supernatural life.
- People with Empires in their Minds rewrite history.
- People with Empires in their Minds expect supernatural Miracles...and double their goals.

Seven Qualities of Dream Makers.

1. *Empires in the mind.*
2. *Energizing relationships.*
3. *Flexibility: A readiness to make radical moves.*
4. *A willingness to ignore Fools.*
5. *Confidence and knowledge of your dominant gift.*
6. *A picture of the future you are unwilling to live without.*
7. *An obsession with somebody's success.*

So, leave the past behind. Let go of yesterday. The only place yesterday is happening is in your mind. Embrace a new beginning. The future you've been dreaming about is here now, not there and then!

Second Sunday in August

ONE-YEAR BIBLE PLAN: PSALM 94-96/ ROMANS 9:17-33

CONGREGATIONAL EVANGELISM 1/3

1. Evangelism is to be a central feature of the Church.

   a. To make disciples of all the nations – Matt. 28:19-20.

   b. To preach the gospel to every person – Mk. 16:15-16.

2. There are many good ways to evangelize.

   a. Public preaching and teaching, private studies and conversations, TV, radio, the Internet, and Social Media.

   b. What works well often depends on the circumstances and culture, etc.

3. What works well in many places can be described as "Congregational Evangelism."

   a. Assuming there is a congregation that already exists in a community.

   b. Assuming its members will do their part to make it work. "Congregational Evangelism" could describe many local churches' efforts.

I will use congregational Evangelism to describe one particular approach in the next lesson in this series.

Memory Verse: Mark 16:15: *"And he said unto them, Go ye into all the world, and preach the gospel to every creature."*

Monday, August 12th

ONE-YEAR BIBLE PLAN: PSALM 97-99/ ROMANS 10:1-21

Psalm 40:1-4: *".... He brought me up out of a horrible pit, out of the miry clay, set my feet upon a rock, and established my goings. And he hath put a new song in my mouth, even ..."*

A NEW SONG

Saint, is your life a tale of demonic oppression, depression, and suppression? Are you heavily indebted? Are you in some satanic bondage? Are you living in poverty, joblessness, loneliness, sickness, bareness, and other afflictions? Has the devil placed you in any of the above categories? Hear ye the counsel of God: *You are coming out of this satanic categorization this day in Jesus' Name!*

A pit of miry clay represents all and more of the above-listed situation. Miry clay is the slippery, sticky part of soil [earth]. It is naturally found in a swampy area or underneath a waterlogged area. When a vehicle is trapped in clay, it requires extra and external effort to get out.

In the realm of the spirit, miry clay symbolizes terrible life situations that trap and stall people's progress. When you are in miry clay, you find it difficult to make significant advances in all spheres of life. You work so hard with little or no results. Such hindrances could manifest in the form of health challenges, debits, miscarriages, etc., which culminate in making life unbearable. It is impossible to come out of miry clay without divine intervention. *Today, the Almighty God will divinely intervene in your situation in the Name of Jesus Christ. Amen!*

Prayer: *Father, put a new song in my mouth today!*

Tuesday, August 13th

ONE-YEAR BIBLE PLAN: PSALM 100-102/ ROMANS 11:1-18

Psalm 91:7-10: *"A thousand shall fall at thy side, and ten thousand at thy right hand, but it shall not come nigh thee. No evil shall befall thee; neither shall any plague come nigh thy dwelling."*

NO EVIL

It is a terrifying world we're living in today. A world that staggers from one disaster to another. Almost daily, we hear about wars, the dangers of nuclear weapons and chemical warfare, oil spills and earthquakes, fire and floods, diseases on the rise, and crime sweeping through our cities. But in the midst of it all, God promises to be a refuge and a fortress to those who will trust and dwell in Him.

But you might say, *"He made that promise thousands of years ago when things weren't in as desperate shape as they are today!"* But that promise was made for our generation also. Because when **Psalm 91** was written, man hadn't even invented weapons that could destroy 5,000 people at once. We did that. So, when He said, "No evil will befall you," He included us.

No evil will b52efall you. Hold on to it, and believe it today. Believe that God wants to be God in your life. He wants to be your protection. He wants to be your security. He wants to be the first name you call when trouble comes your way. He wants to be the One you trust in and look to keep you safe. And if you do that, He'll never let you down.

Prayer: *I decree no evil shall befall me in Jesus' Name. Amen!*

Wednesday, August 14th

ONE-YEAR BIBLE PLAN: PSALM 103-105/ROMANS 11:19-36

CONGREGATIONAL EVANGELISM 3/3

B. BY ACTIVATING THE CONGREGATION'S SERVICES: The members of the church assembly must endeavor to arrive early to every meeting. Visitors usually arrive early and plan to leave early.

The members must endeavor to greet the visitors: Greet them in the parking lot. Greet them before services begin. If a welcoming committee is assigned, apart from ushers, they should sit in the back rows of the church.

The members must offer worship that edifies: By those who lead, setting the example with enthusiasm **1st Corinthians 14:24-26.**

ENTHUSIASM STARTS WITH:

- Those who make the announcements.
- Continuing with those who lead in song and prayer.
- And, of course, the Sunday School teacher and the preacher!

Every member also set an example:

- By how they sing or do not sing – **1st Cor. 14:15.**
- By how they pray and say "Amen" – **1st Corinthians 14:15-16.**
- By how they listen with readiness or boredom. - **Acts 17:11.**

The members must 'meet and greet' the visitors After services, if not before.

Visitors must be given priority over other members: You can always greet the members later. This may be your only opportunity with the visitor.

Always consider when a visitor leaves our services, what will they think?

Will they want to return?

- o   Hopefully, their experience will encourage them to return, where there will be an opportunity to learn more about what they think of our assembly.
- o   Where opportunities for personal study will be more likely.
- o   Eventually, the gospel is shared and gratefully received!

Congregational Evangelism," as defined in this study, is nothing more than:

- o   The congregation members use their contacts to invite people to services.
- o   Ensure those who visit are encouraged by what they see to return.
- o   When this happens, the opportunity to sow the seed of the gospel will be greatly enhanced.

Memory Verse: 1ˢᵗ Corinthians 14:23: *"How is it then, brethren? When ye come together, every one of you hath a psalm, a doctrine, a tongue, a revelation, an interpretation. Let all things be done unto edifying."*

Thursday, August 15th

ONE-YEAR BIBLE PLAN: PSALM 106-108/ROMANS 12:1-21

Hebrews 11:1: *"Now faith is the substance of things hoped for, the evidence of things not seen."*

THE NOW FAITH

So often, we have faith in the future. We believe "one day" God is going to do something great. "One day," we'll get a good break. "One day," we'll feel better. "One day," the problem will turn around. It's good to have faith in the future and believe that God will take care of us, but we can become so future-minded that we lose sight of the fact that God wants to do something great in our lives today.

Today, God wants to show you His favor. Today, God wants to amaze you with His goodness. He is called "the Great I Am," not "the Great I Was" or "the Great I Will Be." God is always in the present, and true faith is always in the present. Faith in the future is good, but you must start releasing your faith for now. The Bible says, *"Now faith is."* The faith that's alive and active is your faith for today. Every day, get up with that mentality, "Something good is going to happen to me today!"

Prayer:

Father, today I ask for a breakthrough. I pray that You will send a favor today. I pray that You will send restoration today. I pray that You will send healing today. I thank You in advance for Your goodness and grace today and every day of my life in Jesus' Name. Amen!

Friday, August 16th

ONE-YEAR BIBLE PLAN: PSALM 109-111/ ROMANS 13:1-14

Ephesians 3:16 TLB: *"Out of his glorious, unlimited resources, he will give you the mighty inner strengthening of his Holy Spirit."*

NO COMPROMISE

Horace Pitkin, the son of a wealthy merchant, was converted and went to China as a missionary. He wrote to his friends in America, saying, *"It will be but a short time till we know definitely whether we can serve Him better above or here."*

Shortly afterward, a mob stormed the compound gate where Pitkin defended the women and children. He was beheaded and offered his head at the shrine of a heathen god while his body was thrown into a pit with the bodies of nine Chinese Christians.

Sherwood Eddy, writing about him, said, *"Pitkin won more men by his death than he ever could have won by his life."*

Christ needs people today who are made of martyr stuff!

Dare to take a strong, uncompromising stand for Him.

Saint, you are not worth what you receive if you don't support your belief.

Prayer:

Thank You, Lord, for the examples of those who have gone before us. Help me to take hold of Your unlimited strength, too.

Saturday, August 17th

ONE-YEAR BIBLE PLAN: PSALM 112-114/ ROMANS 14:1-23

WISDOM OF THE ORACLE

A SIMPLIFIED LIFE 1/2

- **Any movement towards order creates pleasure.** So many people are running around in circles, and everything still needs to be done.

- **Once we learn a valuable secret**...how to organize our world and simplify our lives, we start accomplishing things!

- **We must continually be in the process of organizing our world and simplifying our lives.** Then goals will be met, and Dreams fulfilled.

- **Order is the accurate arrangement of things.** There are some important facts we should remember about organization and order.

- **Order is a customized thing.** What you consider the most important is for you and not for anybody else.

- **Organizing your world means deciding between what is important and what is not important.** What needs to be accessible and seen? What needs to be out of sight but referenceable? These are decisions.

Third Sunday in August

ONE-YEAR BIBLE PLAN: PSALM 115-117/ ROMANS 15:1-16

FOLLOW-UP 1/12

In the Great Commission, in **Matthew 28,** Jesus did not simply tell His apostles to baptize the new converts; He said, *"teaching them to observe all things that I have commanded you."* **Matthew 28:19-20.**

He wanted them to 'follow up' with those who were baptized. Too often, once people are baptized, they are left to drift.

In many cases, they drift back into the world. Or they drift into apathy regarding their devotion and service to God.

This greatly hinders the growth of the Lord's Church: Not only are the souls who drift in danger of falling away. We must think of the potential souls they could have brought to the Lord if they had been faithful!

So, proper 'follow-up' should be paramount to any congregation.

> **Memory Verse: Matthew 28:19-20:** *"Go ye therefore, and teach all nations, baptizing them in the name of the Father, and of the Son and the Holy Ghost: Teaching them to observe all things whatsoever I have commanded you: and, lo, I am with you always, even unto the end of the world. Amen."*

Monday, August 19th

ONE-YEAR BIBLE PLAN: PSALM 118-120/ROMANS 15:17-33

2nd Kings 4:8-17: *"And he said, about this season, according to the time of life, thou shalt embrace a son. And she said, Nay, my lord, thou man of God, do not lie unto thine handmaid...."*

INVOLVE IN GOD

Supporting kingdom work without prompting is a major factor in the process of getting uncommonly blessed. Positioning yourself to discover the kingdom's needs and that of God's servants provokes God to do deeds that meet all your needs. The fact that you always supply God's needs without duress qualifies you to receive miracles without asking.

This is exactly what happened to the Shunamite woman in the scripture above. She offered her home, food services, etc., without request, to the 'Oracle of God' Elisha. Making herself an agent of spreading the gospel, she positioned herself in God's heart for uncommon miracles.

I may not know your vocation, you may be pursuing a career, or you may even be unemployed; I admonish you this day, whatever you are involved in, you must involve God in it; let Him be your senior partner. The Lord acknowledges anyone who selflessly invests their talent, time, energy, funds, etc., to advance kingdom work as His partner. When you grab this vision and run with it, your cup of blessings runs over. Have you been contributing your resources towards kingdom work? *Beloved, be expectant, for God is about to surprise you this season.*

Prayer: *Lord, give me the grace to be more involved in You!*

Tuesday, August 20th

ONE-YEAR BIBLE PLAN: PSALM 121-123/ ROMANS 16:1-13

2nd Corinthians 12:9: *"And he said unto me, My grace is sufficient for thee: my strength is perfect in weakness...."*

PERFECT STRENGTH

When you run into a situation you don't have the strength or the ability to handle, are you often tempted to give up and accept defeat? Don't! Instead, shout, "Glory!" because God's strength is about to be made perfect in you.

The word translated as "strength" in this scripture is Dunamis. It means "God's miracle-working power." Just think about that. When your human strength ends, God has promised His miraculous power will bring you through!

In **Acts 14,** Paul was stoned by some Jews, taken out of the city, and left for dead. Paul's human strength had ended. He was powerless. But the disciples gathered around him and prayed, the Lord raised him, and he went on his way.

In other words, when Paul didn't have enough strength to overcome, God's miracle-working power was sufficient for him. It enabled him to be an overcomer despite his weakness!

So, if you are facing a crisis today—If you're sick and medicine has failed you—If your debts are out of control—If your family is falling apart—If bad habits have you hopelessly bound—If you've done absolutely all you know to do and you still haven't gotten results—Then rejoice! For when we fail, the power of God excels! Only believe! God's grace is sufficient for you!

Wednesday, August 21st

ONE-YEAR BIBLE PLAN: PSALM 124-126/ROM. 16:14-27

FOLLOW-UP 2/12

DEFINITION OF FOLLOW-UP:

A. THE WORK OF GROUNDING A NEW BELIEVER: We notice as an important part of Paul's ministry in **Colossians 1:28-29; Acts 14:21-22 TLB.**

B. FOLLOW-UP INVOLVES SEVERAL AREAS OF SPIRITUAL GROWTH:

1. Having the assurance of salvation and acceptance by God – **1st John 5:13; 1st John 2:3.**

2. Developing a consistent devotional life – **1st Peter 2:2 AMPC; MSG; Colossians 4B; MSG.**

3. Understanding the basics of abundant Christian living - **Colossians 3:12-17 AMPC; 2nd Peter 1:5-11 AMPC**

4. We are integrating into the family life of the local church - **Hebrews 10:24-25.**

5. Grounded in the basics of the doctrine of Christ - **Hebrews 5:12; Hebrews 6:1-3.**

6. Getting involved in sharing the gospel – **1st Peter 2:9-10.**

> **Memory Verse: Hebrews 5:12:** *"For when for the time ye ought to be teachers, ye have need that one teach you again which be the first principles of the oracles of God; and are become such as require milk, and not of strong meat."*

Thursday, August 22nd

ONE-YEAR BIBLE PLAN: PSALM 127-129/ 1ST COR. 1:1-16

Galatians 6:7-8: *"Do not be deceived, God is not mocked; for whatever a man sows, he will also reap. For he who sows to his flesh will of the flesh reap corruption, but he who sows to the Spirit will of the Spirit reap everlasting life."*

SOW TO THE SPIRIT

Life is full of choices. We need to think about our choices and what the consequences of our choices are -corruption or eternal life!

Some delude themselves into thinking that God does not know the carnal desires of their hearts or the ungodly imaginations that lurk in the shadows of their minds. But Paul clarifies that our ungodly ways and secret sins do not mock God. All sins begin in the thought life. When a temptation comes up as a thought and is accepted, it gives birth to sin, and when sin is full grown [practiced], it brings forth death **James 1:14-15.** This death is reaping the wages of sin- a spiritual death.

Only Jesus can free us from all of this and make us free! **John 8:34-36.** So, why not choose life and avoid suffering and misery? Sow to the Spirit and reap eternal life!

Paul tells us that to be spiritually minded is life and peace **Romans 8:6.** If we walk in the Spirit, we will not fulfill the lusts of the flesh **Galatians 5:16-17.** May we learn the lesson of sowing and reaping in our lives and avoid walking into trouble by our actions and choices.

Prayer: *Lord, give the grace to sow in the spirit!*

Friday, August 23rd

ONE-YEAR BIBLE PLAN: PSALM 130-132/ 1ST COR. 1:17-31

Psalm 100:2: *"Serve the LORD with gladness: come before his presence with singing."*

SERVE THE LORD INTENTIONALLY

When Jesus rode triumphantly into Jerusalem, He knew He would be arrested and condemned. Yet He still went because He was ready to lay down His life. He did it intentionally! It was a strategic move. He decided to lay down His life for us because He loved us. But He will never force anyone to serve Him.

Many have asked: Why didn't God stop Adam from eating the forbidden fruit? God gave him the power of choice. And God will always respect your choice. So, choose to serve Him with all you have. He has shown you mercy and Grace. If you are still waiting to be persuaded before you serve, then you don't love Him. The Psalmist said, *"Serve the Lord with gladness."* Be happy and grateful to serve.

If you appreciate the price He paid you, your attitude will differ. He died for your sins! He said you shouldn't go to hell. But it's a choice! You can choose to become a drunkard and drink yourself into a stupor daily. You can even choose to sniff some kinds of stuff. He will still be looking at you. But if you love your Master, you will not abuse your body. Why won't you serve God? You were a disaster going somewhere to happen. But He saw you and saved you! So, you must decide to serve God if you love Him and appreciate His loving kindness and goodness towards you.

Prayer: *I pledge to serve the Lord with gladness!*

Saturday, August 24th

ONE-YEAR BIBLE PLAN: PSALM 133-135/ 1ST COR. 2:1-16

WISDOM OF THE ORACLE

A SIMPLIFIED LIFE 2/2

- **You must simplify your day before you can simplify your World.**

- **You decide how you want it to begin and how you want it to end.** You cannot decide every event of the day, but there are two things you can decide. What you do first and what you do last.

- **Manage the parts of your life that you can control.** Manage the hours of your life that you can control.

- **Do whatever it takes to keep you motivated.** Do whatever it takes to keep you energized.

- **Identify distractions and deal with them ruthlessly.** Organizing your life will require time, assistance, decision-making, contemplation, eliminating lesser tasks, and prioritizing.

- **It is deadly to have a disorganized life;** a disorganized life is a disorganized world. The tasks with the greatest rewards will be undone.

- **It would be best if you took the time to organize your life,** creating a more simplified and peaceful life, something we should all strive for each day.

Fourth Sunday in August

ONE-YEAR BIBLE PLAN: PSALM 136-138/1ST COR. 3:1-12

FOLLOW-UP 3/12

DEFINITION OF FOLLOW-UP:

C. UTILIZING A THREEFOLD APPROACH:

1. Group follow-up: Nurturing the believer through the local church - **Hebrews 10:25.**

2. Personal study: Activities in which the New Christian engages independently – **1st Timothy 4:13-16.**

3. Personal follow-up: One-to-one relationship with a mature believer to aid and inspire the New Christian's growth - e.g., **Barnabas and Mark, Paul and Timothy.**

This work is best done by members serving as mentors and role models. It should also be done with discretion, e.g., especially following up with women.

With this understanding of 'follow-up,' let's consider some reasons regarding the importance of follow-up.

Memory Verse: Hebrews 10:25: *"Not forsaking the assembling of ourselves together, as the manner of some is but exhorting one another: and so much the more, as ye see the day approaching."*

Monday, August 26th

ONE-YEAR BIBLE PLAN: PSALM 139-141/ ROM. 14:1-23

Luke 18:35-40: "....*and he cried, saying, Jesus, thou son of David, have mercy on me....*"

BE SPIRITUALLY SENSITIVE

The spiritually sensitive Blind Bartimaeus knew exactly what to say to crave the indulgence of the Lord and Savior Jesus Christ and obtain the mercy he desired. He could have continually screamed Jesus of Nazareth, opened my eyes, restored my sight, healed me, among other things that would have had little or no implications or impact. But he cried, *"Jesus of Nazareth, have mercy on me."*

Bartimaeus must have known that mercy overrides all sin and justice. He must have realized that mercy understands, sympathizes, and forgives. He knew mercy was the only thing that could easily touch the heart of God to make the Lord Break protocol. And he received his heart's desire according to his faith. *I prophesy... you will receive your heart's desire according to your faith!*

Beloved, what is it that you desire? Is it healing, breakthrough, favor, blessing, deliverance name it? Whatever it may be that you desire, you can have it if you appropriate the mercy of God. Is the tale of your life stale? Are you struggling with life issues and chain problems? *The Lord is about to take away the struggles, the sufferings, and the reproaches out of your life by His mercy upon you in Jesus' name!* But you must ask to receive, so ask for God's mercy on your heart's desire.

Prayer: *O Lord, have mercy on today in Jesus' Name.*

Tuesday, August 27th

ONE-YEAR BIBLE PLAN: PSALM 142-144/ ROM. 15:1-16

2nd Timothy 1:7: *"For God hath not given us the spirit of fear; but of power, love, and a sound mind."*

FREE OF FEAR

Would you believe me if I said you could be perfectly at peace with fear despite what you see on the news nightly? Fear isn't just a reaction to external circumstances. It's a spiritual force. It begins inside of you. And it is destructive. Fear is Satan's primary weapon. He moves in response to fear, the way God moves in response to faith. Satan challenges the promises of God with it.

In **Matthew 14:30,** Jesus invited Peter to come to Him on the water. *"But when he [Peter] saw the wind boisterous, he was afraid; and beginning to sink, he cried, saying, Lord, save me."* What enabled Peter to walk on the water? His faith in the Word of Jesus. What caused Peter to sink? He saw the wind boisterous, and he was afraid. It wasn't the wind that defeated him; it was his fear of it! He looked at his circumstances and gave in to fear. If Peter had focused on Jesus, his faith would never have wavered. All the blustering and blowing in the world couldn't have drowned him.

Faith is developed by meditating on God's Word. Fear is developed by meditating on Satan's lies. Such fearful meditation is called "worrying." Please don't do it! The Word of God is the sword of the Spirit. Use it to fight Satan every time he comes against you. Hold up your shield of faith and quench all of his fiery darts. *Hallelujah!*

Wednesday, August 28th

ONE-YEAR BIBLE PLAN: PSALM 145-147/1ST COR. 3:13-23

FOLLOW-UP 4/12

II. IMPORTANCE OF FOLLOW-UP

A. VULNERABILITY OF A NEW CHRISTIAN: New believers are vulnerable to the devil's device—**2nd Corinthians 2:11.**

Satan seeks to destroy those in the faith – **1st Peter 5:8-9.**

A Christian is most vulnerable when not grounded in the faith - **Luke 8:13 TLB; AMPC.**

Weak Christians need to be assisted by older, mature Christians - **Galatians 6:1-2 TLB.**

B. POTENTIAL FOR CHANGE IN A NEW CHRISTIAN: A New Convert has expressed godly sorrow and repentance – **2nd Corinthians 7:10 TLB; MSG.**

The desire to change and do what is right is at a peak - **e.g., Acts 16:14-15.**

Given proper direction at this time, much progress can be accomplished – **2nd Corinthians 7:11-13 AMPC, MSG.**

Yet, discouragement and apathy can develop if the desire to change is not cultivated. Therefore, we need to encourage the transformation process for the New Christian.

Memory Verse: 2nd Corinthians 2:11: *"Lest Satan should get an advantage of us: for we are not ignorant of his devices."*

Thursday, August 29th

ONE-YEAR BIBLE PLAN: PSALM 148-150/1ST COR. 4:1-21

Proverbs 14:30 NIV: *"A heart at peace gives life to the body, but envy rots the bones."*

A PEACEFUL HEART

The best thing you can do for health is to set your heart at peace with God. Peace is such a powerful position. It is a position of life and strength. Peace means *"to set at one again."* In other words, we have peace when our minds and hearts are *"at one"* with the Word of God.

It's so easy to let the pressures and distractions of life pull our thoughts away from our heavenly Father. It doesn't take long before we are so focused on earthly things that we feel overwhelmed and stressed. We weren't meant to live filled with anxieties; we were meant to live in peace.

Keep your heart at peace today by staying focused on God the Father. Sow life to your body by agreeing with Him and His Word. Let His peace guard your heart so that you can be equipped to live the abundant life He has promised to you!

Prayer:

"Father, thank You for Your Word, life to my soul. I praise You because You are the Prince of Peace. I choose to set my heart and mind on You today. Thank You for guiding my every step in Jesus' Name! Amen."

Friday, August 30th

ONE-YEAR BIBLE PLAN: PROVERBS 1-3/1ST COR. 5:1-13

Matthew 3:8 AMPC: *"Bring forth fruit consistent with repentance [let your lives prove your change of heart]."*

INSIDE OUT

Our society places so much importance on how things look that appearances often take priority over true quality.

I once saw some big, perfect-looking oranges at the grocery store and decided to buy one. I was sure the orange would taste as good as it looked, but it was dry and bitter when I peeled that beautiful thing and took a bite.

Considering whether you're as good on the inside as you look on the outside is a serious matter. Many people are searching for God today, and there are countless teachings about how to find Him. That sounds right. That's why when people are attracted to your fruit, you must ensure it tastes as good as it looks. Only then will people see Jesus in you and realize He loves them and is the true God.

Prayer:

Father, please show me where I need to take inventory of the fruit in my life; help me fix anything inside that isn't what it needs to be. Thank You for giving me the grace to be authentic and genuinely like You, inside and out. In Jesus' Name, Amen.

Saturday, August 31st

ONE-YEAR BIBLE PLAN: PROVERBS 4-6/ 1ST COR. 6:1-20

WISDOM OF THE ORACLE

MIRACLE

- **Everyone Needs A Miracle.** We ask God for Supernatural Favor, debt cancellation, Reconciliation of homes, and Divine healing. God is a God of Miracles. He never intended for us to live without Miracles.
- **God Gives You A Picture of Your Future That Will Require Miracles.** For you to get from your present to your future with a Miracle, you have yet to see the God-Future for you. The life of Elisha, the Protégé of Elijah, is a remarkable story of a persistent young man who loved Miracles. He loved Miracles so much that he left his Comfort Zone...what he was accustomed to...to pursue the Anointing of his Mentor, Elijah. **1st Kings 19:19-21.**
- **You will never attain God-ordained greatness if you remain in your comfort zone.**
- **You can only have a miracle once you know you need one.**
- **You can only have a Miracle once you know what you do not have.**
- **You have to know what is missing.** That is the first step toward humility, and humility decides what you attract. The moment you say, "There is something I do not have," the Miracle begins.

First Sunday in September

ONE-YEAR BIBLE PLAN: PROVERBS 7-9 / 1ST COR. 7:1-20

FOLLOW-UP 5/12

II. IMPORTANCE OF FOLLOW-UP

C. EFFECTIVE IN PRODUCING SPIRITUAL MULTIPLICATION: Growth in the early church multiplied – **Acts 9:31; Acts 12:24; Acts 6:7.**

'Spiritual multiplication' And 'Spiritual addition':

Spiritual addition - involves leading people to Christ, but that is all.

Spiritual multiplication - involves leading people to Christ and developing them until they lead others to Christ.

'Spiritual multiplication' involves four stages:

1. **Evangelizing** - Teaching others the gospel of Christ - **Matthew 28:19.**

2. **Follow-up** - Teaching them to observe all that Christ commanded - **Matthew 28:20.**

3. **Reproducing** - When they begin to teach others – **2nd Timothy 2:2 TLB.**

4. **Multiplying** - What finally occurs when those taught follow up and make disciples who teach others.

Without 'follow-up,' spiritual multiplication can't occur!

> **Memory Verse: 2nd Timothy 2:2**: *"And the things that thou hast heard of me among many witnesses, the same commit thou to faithful men, who shall be able to teach others also.*

Monday, September 2nd

ONE-YEAR BIBLE PLAN: PROVERBS 10-12/ 1ST COR. 7:21-40

Psalm 67:6-7: *"... Then shall the earth yield her increase..."*

PRAISE GOD AND BE DELIVERED

In **[Acts 16:25-26],** Paul and Silas praised God, and the Lord sent an earthquake to deliver them. Their chains were broken, and the gates of the prison fell flat. Do you desire deliverance? Praise God now!

PRAISE THE LORD NOW!

Lord! I give You all glory and honor. You are worthy of all my praise. Glory to Your Holy Name; I magnify Your Holy Name. You are worthy of all adoration.

You are the king of kings and the Lord of lords, the Ancient of Days, the I Am that I Am, the unchangeable Lord, the impossibility made possible God, You reverse the irreversible, You never sleep nor slumber. I blessed Your Holy Name! In Jesus' Name, I worship!

BIRTHDAY AND ANNIVERSARY PRAYERS!

Father, I commit September children and those celebrating their marriage this month into Your hands: this is the month of fruitfulness; let them be fruitful. Let their children be productive. Let them be fruitful physically, financially, materially, and spiritually in Jesus' Name. Amen!

Tuesday, September 3ʳᵈ

ONE-YEAR BIBLE PLAN: PROVERBS 13-15 / 1ˢᵀ COR. 8:1-13

1ˢᵗ Corinthians 16:13: *"Be on your guard; stand firm in the faith; be courageous; be strong."*

BE COURAGEOUS

Embrace this day with a heart ready to stand guard, be strong, and live courageously in Christ. Today's scripture is like a spiritual armor, equipping us for the day ahead. C.S. Lewis said, *"Courage is not simply one of the virtues, but the form of every virtue at the testing point."*

Being "on guard" is more than a readiness posture; it's a life stance of proactive faithfulness. It requires us to be attuned to the spiritual realm, ever vigilant against the enemy's schemes.

To "stand firm in the faith" is not just to believe but to root ourselves deeply in the rich soil of God's Word, allowing it to nourish our spirits and fortify our resolve. And when we are told to "be courageous and strong," it goes beyond physical or emotional prowess. It's about being fortified by a faith that has been tested, a hope that is anchored on Jesus Christ, and a love that never fails.

Meditate on: what areas of your life is God calling you to be more vigilant? How can you deepen your faith to stand unswerving, courageous, and strong in Him?

Prayer:

Lord, You are my fortress and my strength. Arm me with discernment, gird me with Your truth, and protect me with Your love. Help me stand firm in the faith in Jesus' Name. Amen!

Wednesday, September 4th

ONE-YEAR BIBLE PLAN: PROVERBS 16-18 / 1ST COR. 9:1-14

FOLLOW-UP 6/12

II. IMPORTANCE OF FOLLOW-UP

D. LET'S SEE WHAT HAPPENS WHEN ONE GRASPS 'THE VISION OF MULTIPLICATION': Matthew 28:19-20. Suppose you develop just one truly 'multiplying Christian' each year, which is not an unreasonable goal. It may not seem like much, but if those 'multiplying Christians' developed one more 'multiplying Christian' each year, the result will amaze you. *Let's see how!*

a) In two years, there would be 4.

b) In five years, there would be 32.

c) In ten years, there would be 1,024.

d) In twenty years, there would be 1,048,576.

e) In thirty-three years, there would be 8,589,934,592.

If you baptized 1,000 a year, in thirty-three years, there only would be 33,000. Not all become 'multiplying Christians'; many don't become multiplying believers because of lack of follow-up!

If we want the Lord's church to grow, we must provide follow-up for new Christians. Proper follow-up involves a congregational and individual effort, especially the latter.

Please, this year, let us prayerfully consider what we can do to provide 'follow-up' for New Christians.

Memory Verse: Matthew 28:20

Thursday, September 5th

ONE-YEAR BIBLE PLAN: PROVERBS 19-21 / 1ST COR. 9:15-27

Matthew 6:33: *"But seek ye first the kingdom of God…"*

POWER SOURCE

A man or a woman who has been focusing all attention on financial gains, business, or social prestige or who has centered all his/her affection on someone; that person will experience a devastating sense of loss when denied the thing that has given their life its meaning. In these tragic moments, the individual recognizes how terribly and completely alone they are.

At that moment, the Holy Spirit may cause the worldly scales to fall from their eyes so that they see clearly for the first time.

They begin to recognize God as the only source of real power and the fountainhead of love and companionship. Don't wait for this to be your situation before you seek God and His kingdom first.

What gives your life meaning? Think about it today decide to seek first the kingdom of God and its right way of doing things, and every other thing will be added to you. *Be blessed!*

Prayer:

From out of the depths, Lord, my eyes have seen that only You are unchanging, eternal love. Help me to put You first in everything I do in Jesus' Name. Amen!

Friday, September 6th

ONE-YEAR BIBLE PLAN: PROVERBS 22-24/ 1ST COR. 10:1-16

Deuteronomy 8:17: *"And thou say in thine heart, My power and the might of mine hand hath gotten me this wealth."*

FORGET NOT YOUR SOURCE

Ecclesiastes 12:1 Says, *"Remember now thy Creator in the days of thy youth, while the evil days come not...."*

It's not news that a champion can become an ex-champion, nor can a blessing become a curse. When God blesses a fellow, and they don't acknowledge Him. the blessing can become a curse. This is because God will not share His glory with any man.

Do you know that some are studying and working harder than you, yet they don't have good results to show for it? Many young people attribute their achievements to their efforts, smartness, wisdom, or talents. It's even worse when performing responsibilities in God's house, where people attribute their achievement in spiritual things to their human strategies, forgetting that God is the source of every victory.

If God doesn't endorse a program/project, the laborers will labor in vain. So, the next time you do something great or achieve something good, don't attribute it to your effort: give God all the glory because He is the One crowning your efforts with success.

Prayer:

Father, please forgive me for taking the glory in Jesus' Name meant for You. Amen!

Saturday, September 7th

ONE-YEAR BIBLE PLAN: PROVERBS 25-27/1ST COR. 10:17-33

SEPTEMBER PRAYER FIRESTORM

Jeremiah 36:9: *"Now in the fifth year of Jehoiakim the son of Josiah, king of Judah, in the ninth month, all the people in Jerusalem and all the people who came from the cities of Judah to Jerusalem proclaimed a fast before the Lord."*

FIRESTORM DELIVERANCE PRAYER

⇒ *Lord, we thank You for bringing us safely to September.*

⇒ *Lord, thank you for bringing us to this month's deliverance firestorm.*

⇒ *We take authority over this month in Jesus' Name.*

⇒ *I cover every day of this month with the Blood of Jesus.*

⇒ *I cover every journey I shall embark upon this month with the blood of Jesus.*

⇒ *All things shall work together for good for me this month, in Jesus' Name.*

⇒ *This month, I will rejoice and be glad in it.*

⇒ *I will possess all my blessings attached to this month.*

⇒ *Every crisis assigned against me this month shall backfire.*

⇒ *September is the first month of remembrance, Lord; remember me this month for good in Jesus' Name.*

⇒ *Every good thing locked up by the devil against me is released by fire in Jesus' Name.*

- ⇒ *This month, I repossess every good thing I have lost.*
- o *Evil altars erected to make me cry this month catch fire.*
- o *Enemies waiting to laugh at me this month, be confounded.*
- o *Powers speaking poverty and infirmities into my destiny, die by fire.*
- o *Powers speaking poverty and infirmities into my destiny, die by fire.*
- o *Father, protect my family and me from evil this month.*
- o *Holy Spirit, deliver me from poverty and infirmity.*
- o *Lord Jesus, protect me and my loved ones wherever we go this month.*
- o *Father, open windows of marvelous opportunities for me this month.*
- o *Father, continually renew the strength of Apostle Stevie Okauru.*
- o *Lord, give wisdom and inspiration to every Oracle of God International Ministry worker.*
- o *Father, bless everyone dedicating their time and resources to this ministry in the Name of Jesus.*
- o *Thank God for the prayer answered!*

Second Sunday in September

ONE-YEAR BIBLE PLAN: PROVERBS 28-31 / 1ST COR. 11:1-17

FOLLOW-UP 7/12

FACTORS AFFECTING FOLLOW-UP

Our "Follow-up: Definition & Importance" study learned that personal follow-up was part of an effort to ground New Believers in Christ. We seek to encourage engagement in this service area in the Lord's work. And there is great joy when we engage in such work – **3rd John 4 AMPC**.

Several factors will affect any effort in personal follow-up. Understanding these factors will help one know more about what is involved in such efforts.

It may also help us understand why so few people engage in it.

For example, one factor affecting personal follow-up is:

I. OUR RELATIONSHIP WITH THE LORD:

A. FOLLOW-UP INVOLVES THE IDEA OF "LIFE TRANSFERENCE": Life transference – is the transferring of things in your life to the life of the New Christian. In other words, the sharing of a lifestyle with the New Believer. **Romans 1:9-12.**

Such as Paul also did with the Thessalonians – **1st Thessalonians 2:8.**

B. OUR WALK WITH THE LORD MUST BE WORTHY OF IMITATION: Otherwise, the New Believer will not likely take us seriously.

Consider the example of Paul in his conduct with the Thessalonians in – **1st Thessalonians 2:10.**

So, he writes as he did to the Philippians in - **Philippians 4:9.**

We should not view Paul as an exception; all mature Christians are worthy of imitation - **Philippians 3:17.**

C. THIS MAY EXPLAIN WHY MANY ARE NOT INVOLVED IN FOLLOW-UP: Perhaps they are not good role models or mentors for "life transference."

Suppose such is the case with us. Then we better get busy growing spiritually. We will unlikely help lead others to their salvation if we are not spiritually mature! – **1st Timothy 4:16.**

Another factor affecting personal follow-up is Our willingness to commit. We shall go deeper in our next lesson.

> **Memory Verse: Philippians 3:17:** *"Brethren, be followers together of me, and mark them which walk so as ye have us for an example."*

Monday, September 9th

ONE-YEAR BIBLE PLAN: ECCLESIASTES 1-3/1ST COR. 11:18-34

Jeremiah 32:26-28: *"Then came the word of the LORD unto Jeremiah, saying, behold, I am the LORD, the God of all flesh: is there anything too hard for me?"*

NEVER TOO HARD FOR GOD

I have often met people who thought and even said that God could not solve their problems. Some years ago, a young man wrote me a letter. In the letter, he said his problem was too difficult for God to solve. Nevertheless, he wrote the letter to give God the last chance to redeem His Name by solving his problem, which was perennial joblessness. I prayed for him, and he got a job within a few hours.

Beloved, does your problem seem like it has defied God? Are you in the category of those who consider their problems too big for God? Are you on the verge of losing hope and committing suicide? Fear not, for your problem is not too hard for God. The God I serve is all-powerful. He is the One who created heaven and earth: the clouds, the birds, fish, seasons, human beings, etc., so nothing is too difficult for Him.

That problem you are facing now is a minute thing in His eyes. He can provide a job for you at the next moment. He can improve your life in one instant. Whatever you want, have faith; your problem is not hard for God. He said in His Word I am the God of all flesh. Is anything too hard for me? I prophesy your heart's desire will not be hard for God.

Prayer: *"Mine is not too hard for the Lord*

Tuesday, September 10th

ONE-YEAR BIBLE PLAN: ECCLESIASTES 4-6/ 1ST COR. 12:1-15

Romans 6:4: *"Therefore, we are buried with him by baptism into death: like as Christ was raised from the dead by the glory of the Father, even so we also should walk in newness of life."*

LIVING IN POWER

As believers, we must live in the New Life God gave Jesus when He raised Him from the dead. The old sinner we once were has died. We've become a New Creation full of the resurrection life of God! But sin, disobedience, and living a selfish, carnal life will keep that resurrection life from flowing out. Sin will separate you from God even though you're born again. Resurrection life will lay dormant in you if you walk in sin.

You can't overcome sin by trying to stop sinning. You overcome it by walking after the New Life God has put within you, spending time in the Word, and praying. As you do, the Spirit of God will enable you to put that sin under your feet.

Remember, the Holy Spirit will not force you, but He'll wait for you to take the initiative. Then, He will strengthen you to follow through with your decision. He will teach you how to walk in the New Life that is on the inside of you. Take the first step today by asking for His help. Say, *"Lord, I desire to experience the power to live this new life daily. By a decision of my heart, I put down the dictates of sin. I declare myself dead to sin in Jesus' Name.*

Prayer: *Lord, empower me to live the New Life!*

Wednesday, September 11th

ONE-YEAR BIBLE PLAN: ECCL. 7-9 / 1ST COR. 12:16-31

FOLLOW-UP 8/12

FACTORS AFFECTING FOLLOW-UP

II. OUR WILLINGNESS TO MAKE A COMMITMENT:

A. PERSONAL FOLLOW-UP IS TIME-CONSUMING: The needs of a New Believer are often like that of a baby [feeding, bonding, protecting]. When life's busy schedule presses down, priorities must be made. Only the truly committed will spend the time necessary to follow up—**Acts 20:20, Acts 20:31, 1st Thessalonians 2:9-12 AMPC.**

B. THIS IS WHY SO FEW ENGAGE IN FOLLOW-UP: Commitment is difficult for many people. Lack of commitment is seen in many areas: work, marriage, family, church, and social club membership. Many lack commitment to save themselves, let alone others!

C. ARE WE ABLE TO MAKE THE COMMITMENT?

Do we believe in the importance of personal follow-up? Are we willing to devote the time necessary to encourage new disciples? Can we rethink our present activities and discontinue those which interfere with our desire to be more committed? Even when we are convinced of the need and are willing to commit, we must be aware of other factors affecting personal follow-up:

Memory Verse: Acts 20:20: *"And how I kept back nothing profitable unto you, but have shewed you, and have taught you publicly, and from house to house."*

Thursday, September 12th

ONE-YEAR BIBLE PLAN: ECCL. 10-12/ 1ST COR. 13:1-13

Acts 18:24: *"This man was instructed in the way of the Lord; and being fervent in the spirit, he spake and taught diligently the things of the Lord, knowing only the baptism of John."*

OTHERS' INPUT

Apollos was eloquent. He was a great preacher. And he was mighty in the scriptures. So, you will expect that he should know everything. But that wasn't the case. He can quote many scriptures, but he cannot apply them. There are people like that today. They can quote many scriptures but may not apply them.

Apollos was diligent and sincere in the things of the Kingdom. But he knew only the Baptism of John. This shows that his knowledge was limited, yet he was mighty in the scriptures. He was very eloquent, teaching and conducting a lot of things. Probably, he had a large followership. But he knew only the baptism of John. That was all he knew. But God brought him in contact with two people who invested in his life and helped him become a better gospel preacher. **Acts 18:26-27.**

Aquila and Priscilla were disciples of Paul, and they had greater insight into the message of Grace than Apollo. There are people that God had planted in your pathway who have deeper insight than you have. Glean from them. If you are open to learning from others, you will improve in whatever you are involved. Hallelujah!

Prayer: *"Lord, divinely connect me with those who lift me!*

Friday, September 13th

ONE-YEAR BIBLE PLAN: S.O.S. 1-3/ 1ST COR. 14:1-20

Hebrews 11:1: *"Now faith is the substance of things hoped for, the evidence of things not seen."*

THE NOW FAITH

So often, we have faith in the future. We believe "one day" God is going to do something great. "One day," we'll get a good break. "One day," we'll feel better. "One day," the problem will turn around. It's good to have faith in the future and believe that God will take care of us, but we can become so future-minded that we lose sight of the fact that God wants to do something great in our lives today.

Today, God wants to favor you. Today, God wants to amaze you with His goodness. He is called "the Great I Am," not "the Great I Was" or "the Great I Will Be." God is always in the present, and true faith is always in the present.

Faith in the future is good, but you must start releasing your faith for now. The Scripture says, "Now faith is." The faith that's alive and active is your faith for today. Every morning, you should get up with the attitude, "Something good is going to happen to me today!"

Prayer:

Father, today I ask for a breakthrough. I pray that You will send a favor today. I pray that You will send restoration today. I pray that You will send healing today. Thank You in advance for Your goodness and grace today and every day of my life, in Jesus' Name! Amen.

Saturday, September 14th

ONE-YEAR BIBLE PLAN: S.O.S. 4-6/ 1ST COR. 14:21-40

WISDOM OF THE ORACLE

COMMENDATION

- It is with humans to commend but with God to approve.
- God's approval is superior to human commendation.
- Craving for commendation will move you to seek to impress others instead of pleasing God.
- Constant desire to obtain commendations can lead to distraction and compromise.
- But it takes focus to please God.
- Pleasing God to secure His approval is the greatest reward of life.
- To hear Him say to you, "Well done," at the end of your vacation on earth is the most honorable and prestigious thing.
- Therefore, focus on your God-given assignment, and you will always succeed.

Third Sunday in September

ONE-YEAR BIBLE PLAN: S.O.S. 7-8/ 1ˢᵀ COR. 15:1-17

FOLLOW-UP 9/12

FACTORS AFFECTING FOLLOW-UP

III. WILLINGNESS TO CONCENTRATE EFFORTS:

A. IT IS TEMPTING TO WORK WITH TOO MANY AT ONE TIME: Because of what others may expect of us, we may think, "We should not be working with just a select few." And because of what may be for our vain glory, "Numbers impress brethren more than quality, so we may wish it is better work with many."

B. GOOD FOLLOW-UP REQUIRES CONCENTRATED FOCUS: Only working with a few at once can work. While multitudes followed Him, Jesus focused on his select disciples during His ministry. Paul told Timothy to work with 'faithful' men – **2ⁿᵈ Timothy 2:2.**

"A decision that our ministry will be intensive rather than extensive will be challenging. Quality begets quantity. It takes vision to train one man to reach the mass." – Waylon Moore.

C. DO WE HAVE THE VISION TO FOCUS OUR EFFORTS? We should be open to encouraging all our brethren. But prime time and peak energy should be directed toward a select few until they can follow up on others.

Memory Verse: 2ⁿᵈ Timothy 2:2: *"And the things that thou hast heard of me among many witnesses, the same commit thou to faithful men, who shall be able to teach others also."*

Monday, September 16th

ONE-YEAR BIBLE PLAN: ISAIAH 1-3/ 1ST COR. 15:18-37

Daniel 5:11-12: *"There is a man in thy kingdom, in whom is the spirit of the holy gods…."*

The passage above is a testament to the queen of Babylon concerning Daniel when the King searched for someone capable of elucidating or decoding 'the handwriting on the wall.' Daniel was assigned to resolve the problem based on this reference, eventually leading to his promotion to the third most powerful person in the land. **Daniel 5:29.**

Beloved, I like you to know that in the affairs of men, the Omnipotent reigneth. You excel above your contemporaries when God releases the spirit of excellence, divine wisdom, knowledge, and uncommon comprehension upon you.

This allows you to live the supernatural life available to you as a member of the Body of Christ. You become a genius as you are born again of the Spirit of God. The level at which you function and your potential become heavenly. You become divinely endowed.

Now Daniel said I have understanding by the book. Which book? This book of the Law, the Word of God, shall not depart from your mouth. Your potential depends on how much you are equipped with God's Word. The more you meditate on the Word of God, the more it permeates your soul and spirit to express God in you. *I pray that you may manifest greatness by the Spirit of the Lord that is released upon you right now in Jesus' name. Amen!*

Prayer: *Lord, permeate me with Your Spirit in Jesus' Name!*

Tuesday, September 17th

ONE-YEAR BIBLE PLAN: ISAIAH 4-6/ 1ST COR. 15:38-58

Matthew 26:2: *"Ye know that after two days is the feast of the Passover, and the Son of man is betrayed to be crucified."*

NO CONDEMNATION

There was a crucifixion in **Genesis 40:19. Deuteronomy 21:22-23** says that anyone hung upon a tree was accursed.

Breaking the law brought on the curse. But Christ has redeemed us from the curse of the law. Through Christ, we will never receive any curse from God even though we somehow disobey the law. Justice was satisfied when Jesus died for the law that we broke, thus paying the penalty and bearing the curse.

No condemnation awaits us from the law, for we died in Him. A Believer who still walks in condemnation is condemned by the devil or himself. God does not condemn us **Romans 8:34.** The law brought God's adverse sentence against us. When the government condemns a building, it is declared unfit for use and must be destroyed. Likewise, when Satan condemns us, he makes us feel unfit for use and ready to be destroyed.

Since the Believer is no longer under the law, they should no longer be condemned or feel unfit for use. The Father has accepted us through Jesus. God convicts of sin but doesn't condemn **Romans 8:34.** Conviction is solely for our profit with no malice, while condemnation includes punishment. Satan is the one who condemns the Christian, but the Holy Spirit has given us the power to escape that condemnation.

Wednesday, September 18th

ONE-YEAR BIBLE PLAN: ISAIAH 7-9/ 1ST COR. 16:1-12

FOLLOW-UP 10/12

FACTORS AFFECTING FOLLOW-UP.

IV. OUR WILLINGNESS TO GO THE DURATION:

A. DEVELOPING DISCIPLES CAN BE A LENGTHY PROCESS: The illustration of 'spiritual multiplication' in our previous study revealed that it takes nearly six years for noticeable growth to occur. Even Jesus spent three years developing His disciples. Paul was in relative obscurity for ten years before he began his missionary journeys.

B. WILLINGNESS TO GO THE DURATION REQUIRES:

1. **Vision** - the same vision Jesus had - **Matthew 13:31-32; Isaiah 60:22.**

2. **Patience** - willing to allow time for spiritual growth and for spiritual multiplication to occur.

C. COULD THIS EXPLAIN WHY SOME DO NOT PERSIST IN THIS WORK? We are a society motivated by "get rich quick" schemes fed by "fast food" restaurants. We want salvation in four or five easy steps and at little cost. However, we must be willing to endure like Jeremiah, who labored for fifty years with little to show for his labors.

Indeed, the fruit of our labors in 'follow-up' may sometimes only show up after we are gone! But we will not grow weary with faith and vision, **Galatians 6:9 TLB.**

> **Memory Verse: Galatians 6:9:** *"And let us not be weary in well doing: for in due season, we shall reap if we faint not."*

Thursday, September 19th

ONE-YEAR BIBLE PLAN: ISAIAH 10-12/ 1ST COR. 16:13-23

1st Chronicles 12:38: *"All these men of war that could keep rank came with a perfect heart to Hebron, to make David king over all Israel: and all the rest also of Israel were of one heart to make David king."*

DIVINE HELPER

1st Chronicles 12:23-40 has a listing of different tribes of Israel who were ready to turn the kingdom from Saul to David. The individuals were of one and perfect heart and were there to accomplish God's plan for David. They were also experts in their own right. While the children of Issachar understood the times and what Israel ought to do, those of Zebulun and Dan were experts in war. The descendants of Naphtali could expertly handle shields and spears. In their thousands, they came to make David the king and were neither mischievous nor crafty about their mission. Interestingly, they were with David for three days, eating and drinking.

It is blessed to have destiny helpers who will defy all odds to support us. Many have lost hope in life, thinking that God has abandoned them. Remember, if thousands of people from different tribes of Israel could be willing to make David king, God can draw people from any corner of the earth to come to your aid, as long as you are within the circle of His will. Pray that He sends such help to enable you to accomplish His purpose.

Prayer: *Lord, send me destiny helpers to help me fulfill my purpose in Jesus' Name. Amen!*

Friday, September 20th

ONE-YEAR BIBLE PLAN: ISAIAH 13-15/2ND COR. 1:1-12

John 4:42: *"... this is indeed the Christ, the world's Savior."*

FOREVER CONNECTED

History, philosophy, theology, and—in many centers of learning—even the sciences are being studied to discover what they have to say about Jesus Christ. The records of the Early Church are being reexamined for their testimony to Him. Archaeologists are digging to discover new evidence.

Some say that Jesus Christ is a myth and never existed in history. Others say that He was merely a man, that there was nothing supernatural about His birth, and that His resurrection was a hallucination. Others talk about a Christless Christianity. Some say that no matter what one thinks about Christ, it does not affect Christianity. They are all wrong!

Christianity is forever linked with the Person of Christ.

Carlyle recognized this when he said, *"Had this doctrine of the deity of Christ been lost, Christianity would have vanished like a dream."*

The historian Lecky remarks, *"Christianity is not a system of morals; it is the worship of a Divine Person Christ."*

Prayer:

Lord Jesus, You are the living Christ I love and revere.

Saturday, September 21st

ONE-YEAR BIBLE PLAN: ISAIAH 16-18/ 2ND COR. 1:13-24

WISDOM OF THE ORACLE

KEEP THE FIRE

- It takes New Wood to re-ignite fresh fire. **Leviticus 6:12-13.**
- Fire goes down where there is no more wood. **Leviticus 26:20.**
- Do not watch your flame turn to ash.
- Ash only leaves a memory of fire, which can be painful to watch while alive.
- The only way to stir up and re-ignite the flame is to get New Wood.
- New Wood is the New Revelation of God's Word.
- New revelation will always spark off fresh revolution of fire.
- Go for the lasting revelation that will sustain your flame of fire. **Leviticus 6:12-13; Proverbs 27:20; Haggai 1:8.**

Fourth Sunday in September

ONE-YEAR BIBLE PLAN: ISAIAH 19-21/ 2ND COR. 2:1-17

FOLLOW-UP 11/12

FACTORS AFFECTING FOLLOW-UP.

A fifth factor affecting follow-up is:

V. OUR WILLINGNESS TO TEACH AND TRAIN:

A. TEACHING OF GOD'S WORD IS REQUIRED: As Paul instructed Timothy in – **2nd Timothy 2:2.**

We were accompanied by our example [which we saw earlier in 'life transference']. Yet the Word ultimately produces spiritual growth and change – **1st Peter 1:23; 1st Peter 2:2.**

B. THIS REQUIRES BEING A FAITHFUL STUDENT: As Paul instructed Timothy in – **1st Timothy 4:15-16.**

Not only for our spiritual growth but to set an example for others – **1st Timothy 4:12.**

C. COULD THIS EXPLAIN THE LACK OF GROWTH IN SOME CONVERTS? What kind of students of God's Word do they see in us? Is our attendance in Bible Study erratic? Do we need to prepare to share? Are we willing to take the time to study with New Converts in person?

Finally, another factor affecting follow-up pertains to our next study in this series:

> **Memory Verse: 1st Timothy 4:12:** *"Let no man despise thy youth; but be thou an example of the believers, in word, in conversation, in charity, in spirit, in faith, in purity."*

Monday, September 23rd

ONE-YEAR BIBLE PLAN: ISAIAH 19-21/ 2ND COR. 3:1-18

Habakkuk 2:1-3: *"……. but at the end, it shall speak, and not lie though it tarry, wait for it; because it will surely come, it will not tarry."*

DELAY IS NOT DENIAL

Delayed gratification makes people lose hope and faith in God. Waiting for your breakthrough and testimonies endlessly, without results, leads to doubt in God's ability to make good His promises. Though God is aware of your shortcomings, He advocates for you to exercise patience in all your expectations as He perfects that which concerns you.

And in God's calendar, a time frame is apportioned to everything. That is what God told Prophet Habakkuk in 'Today's Word.' God gave Habakkuk an insight into the workings and process of release of blessings and breakthroughs, from developing a vision to writing it down and praying them into manifesting.

When you fulfill these conditions, it is just a matter of time for you to receive the manifestation of your heart's desires. And I strongly believe you have some expectations, *so I pray for you this day for a speedy manifestation of your earnest heart desires in Jesus' Name. Amen!*

But you have to write down your desire, take a pen and paper, and write down your dreams; now go further and add a realistic expectation date to your list. Then, begin to work and walk towards achieving those desires. For faith without works is dead.

Tuesday, September 24th

ONE-YEAR BIBLE PLAN: ISAIAH 22-24/ 2ND COR. 4:1-18

Jeremiah 17:7-8: *"But blessed is the one who trusts in the LORD, whose confidence is in him. They will be like a tree planted by the water that sends its roots by the stream..."*

BE PLANTED

As you begin your day, plant your hopes and fears in the nourishing soil of God's promises, for it's in Him that we find the assurance to stand tall and resilient.

C.S. Lewis said, *"In seasons of drought and abundance, our trust in God becomes the defining narrative of our lives."*

In the ebb and flow of life, we often find ourselves in varying seasons – times of abundance and moments of scarcity. The Prophet Jeremiah paints a vivid picture of unwavering faith: a tree unshaken by external circumstances because it is deeply rooted in a perpetual source of life. This isn't about mere survival but thriving, as evidenced by its continuous fruitfulness.

In the same way, anchoring our trust in the Lord allows us to flourish even in the harshest seasons. Our challenges will not define us, but our trust in Him will.

Ask yourself as you mediate today: Am I allowing my circumstances to define me, or is my identity anchored in the Lord? How can I cultivate a steadfast and fruitful heart regardless of life's seasons?

Prayer: *Father, Help me to sink my roots deep into Your love and truth in Jesus' Name. Amen.*

Wednesday, September 25th

ONE-YEAR BIBLE PLAN: ISAIAH 25-27/ 2ND COR. 5:1-10

FOLLOW-UP 12/12

FACTORS AFFECTING FOLLOW-UP.

VI. OUR SPIRITUAL ENVIRONMENT:

A. THE ROLE OF A SPIRITUAL ENVIRONMENT FOR A NEW CHRISTIAN: This plays a large part in their spiritual growth. A lukewarm or cold church environment can devastate a New Believer's growth. It can hinder or hurt the efforts of the faithful few trying to nurture new Christians.

B. EFFECTIVE FOLLOW-UP MAY FIRST REQUIRE CLEANUP: Working first with those who have poor examples will only undermine future efforts. And then spending time and effort to ensure the local congregation will be a haven for New Believers.

C. COULD THIS EXPLAIN THE LACK OF GROWTH IN SOME CONVERTS? A faithful few may try to follow up with New Believers or members. But are their efforts impacted negatively by the poor examples being set by others?

The work of **personal follow-up** is a challenging task. Which may explain why it is so greatly neglected.

Which is why we need to accept the challenge.

For those willing to accept the task of personal follow-up.

- They will help the church 'multiply' - **Acts 9:31.**
- They will experience 'no greater joy' – **3rd John 4.**

- And they will become imitators of the household of Stephanas: *"They have devoted themselves to the ministry of the saints."* **1st Corinthians 16:15.**

What a wonderful compliment!

Memory Verse: 3rd John 4: *"I have no greater joy than to hear that my children walk in truth."*

Thursday, September 26th

ONE-YEAR BIBLE PLAN: ISAIAH 28-30/ 2ND COR. 5:11-20

2nd Corinthians 5:19: *"God was in Christ, reconciling the world unto himself, not imputing their trespasses unto them; and hath committed unto us the word of reconciliation."*

TELL OTHERS

Many have not heard the "Good News." Because too many believers are telling them God is mad at them and that they're terrible. That's not the "Good News" that God commissioned us to share. He's given us the "word of reconciliation"! He's sent us to tell the news that God has restored harmony and fellowship between Himself and men.

All men. Not just believers. Not just the people in your Church, but everyone! The worst old reprobate sinner in the world is every bit as reconciled to God as you are. Look at **Romans 5:10,** and you'll see what I mean. It says, *"When we were enemies, we were reconciled to God by the death of his Son."*

Reconciled is in the past tense. God has already restored fellowship between Himself and the world. He did it when the entire world was lying in sin. Through the death and resurrection of Jesus, God cleansed, forgiven, and restored to Himself every man, woman, and child on the face of this earth. All any of us have to do now is receive it. That's the good word God has given us. That's the word we need to share with those who are lost. If we do it, I can almost guarantee you, they won't stay lost very long.

Prayer: *Lord, give me the grace to share Your Good Word!*

Friday, September 27th

ONE-YEAR BIBLE PLAN: ISAIAH 31-33/ 2ND COR. 6:1-18

Jonah 3:1-10: *"Now the word of the LORD came to Jonah the second time, saying, "Arise, go to Nineveh, that great city, and preach to it the message that I tell you."*

MESSAGE OF REPENTANCE

God did send Jonah again to deliver the same message he was given earlier. Though Jonah disobeyed initially this time, he delivered God's message very raw to the people of Nineveh and gave them a specific time the judgment of God would come upon them if they failed to repent **verse 4.** Hearing the message, the city repented and put on sack clothes and ashes.

Today, the Church and nations need a raw message from men and women of God. Enough of prosperity messages!

Men and women of God should preach messages that will convict sinners and make sinners afraid to sin. Again, our repentance must be genuine. Nineveh's repentance was genuine, and God heard their cry and had compassion for them. No wonder Jesus made mention of Nineveh's repentance in **Matthew 12:41.**

Prayer:

Dear Lord, give us the heart of repentance as You did for Nineveh in the Name of Jesus Christ. Amen!

Saturday, September 28th

ONE-YEAR BIBLE PLAN: ISAIAH 34-36/ 2ND COR. 7:1-16

WISDOM OF THE ORACLE

EFFECTIVE LEADING

- Effective and productive leaders lead by Strategies.
- Strategy is about approach.
- The approach determines the quality of results.
- Improve your strategy to enhance your results.
- Improve your strategy to reduce your struggles.
- Improve your strategy to enhance your productivity.
- The strategy makes life dynamic.
- It will deliver you from the status quo.

The strategy must be developed primarily in these areas:

- In thinking and planning.
- In implementation and application
- By initiative-focused thinking.
- By continuously evolving and constantly reviewing.
- By developing relationships and leading people to carry out strategically devised plans.
- Get strategic to end triumphantly.

Fifth Sunday in September

ONE-YEAR BIBLE PLAN: ISAIAH 37-39/ 2ND COR. 8:1-12

PREPARING FOR GROW 1/4

Not all churches are prepared to grow numerically and spiritually. Let's consider the church at Laodicea in – **Revelation 3:15-19, Job 22:22-25, Isaiah 55:1, Isaiah 55:11.**

Even if a successful evangelist came and converted many, how many would have remained faithful in such a place?

For churches to grow, they must look beyond their evangelistic efforts. Unless a congregation is prepared to nurture New Converts, any success in evangelism may be short-lived.

To have real, enduring growth, we must get ready to grow!

- We must prepare ourselves as a congregation.
- We must also prepare ourselves individually.

So, what is necessary in "Getting Ready to Grow"?

I. WHAT WE MUST DO AS A CONGREGATION:

A. OFFER ASSEMBLIES THAT EDIFY: The first exposure many have to the gospel is visiting a local congregation.

- **What do they see and hear in the church?**
- **Do they see love in the church? – John 13:34-35.**
- **Does what we do in the church draw people closer to God? – 1st Corinthians 14:25; Genesis 28:16-17.**
- **Do our visitors experience courtesy, warmth, and interest in spiritual matters?**

Not all churches provide the right environment conducive to worship and spiritual growth – 1st Corinthians 11:17 NIV; 1st Corinthians 14:26.

New converts often depend heavily upon the spiritual nourishment provided by the assemblies, and rightly so. As the New Converts get excited by their Newfound Faith, they are anxious to grow quickly and attend all church services. – **Hebrews 10:24-25.**

But if they find half-hearted services?

- o   Praise and worship that is horrible and Dead prayer live.
- o   Members come late to service.
- o   And Old Members barely attend service regularly.

They get discouraged and give up. They may not want to invite other people to the church. Even if they continue to come, they will soon be like the older members.

If we are serious about growing, those who lead us in our assemblies will take their tasks seriously.

1. Coming prepared to serve their role. Doing so gladly and with enthusiasm.

2. Every member will do what they can to make our assemblies edifying to all and everyone.

2. We come early to welcome visitors.

3. Are we participating wholeheartedly in the singing, prayers, and responding to teaching and preaching, etc.? Are we visiting afterward?

Memory Verse: 1st Corinthians 14:26.

Monday, September 30th

ONE-YEAR BIBLE PLAN: ISAIAH 40-42/ 2ND COR. 8:13-24

Psalm 107:1 NIV: *"Give thanks to the LORD, for he is good; his love endures forever."*

In **Matthew 14:15-21**, 5000 men were very hungry. The only food available was a little boy's lunch, yet 12 baskets of bread and fish were left over when the story ended. Between, definitely not enough to more than sufficient lies one sentence – Jesus took the bread and the fish in His hands, and said, "Father, I thank You." *I prophesy that your austerity is changing to prosperity as you thank God now!*

THANKSGIVING PRAYERS!

Father, I thank You! Jehovah, El Shaddai, the God that is more than enough; I thank You! Jehovah Jireh, the Great Provider, I thank You! God of plenty and abundance, I thank You! The Lord who can bring water out of the rock, I thank You! God, who can turn too little into too much?

Thank You! The earth is Yours and the fullness thereof, so I thank You! Silver and Gold are Yours, so I thank You! The cattle upon a thousand hills are all Yours, so I thank You!

The Controller of Heaven and Earth! I give You glory and adoration! The Unchangeable Lord, I thank You! The same yesterday, today, and forever; I thank You! Thank you! King of Glory! I bless Your Holy Name! God of multiplication, I thank You! Father, I thank You from the bottom of my heart! In Jesus' Mighty Name, Amen!

Tuesday, October 1st

ONE-YEAR BIBLE PLAN: ISAIAH 43-45/ 2ND COR. 9:1-15

Psalm 33:1 AMPC: *"Rejoice in the Lord, O you [uncompromisingly] righteous [you upright, in right standing with God]; for praise is becoming and appropriate for those who are upright [in heart]."*

PRAISE GOD

Praise is the most appropriate thing that a believer can do. But God's idea of "appropriate" praise and yours may differ. The praise He calls for is joyous and uninhibited. And, at times, it's just plain loud! If you don't believe it, look in the Bible and see the kind of praise in heaven. **Read Isaiah 6** and find wout how they act in the throne room. The seraphim shout until the doorposts quake! And when they do, the glory of the Lord fills the place. When you get to heaven, you will praise like that, too. You'll be leaping and praising God with every part of your being. But don't wait until then to start. Begin now. Begin to release praises joyously, uninhibitedly. Don't wait until you get to heaven to praise God with all your being. Please do it now.

PRAISE GOD NOW

BIRTHDAY AND ANNIVERSARY PRAYER!

October is the tenth month of the year; ten is two times five, so ten is the number for double grace. Father, I thank You for Your children born in October and those wedded and wedding this month. Thank You for preserving their lives. Lord, release upon them double grace; let their blessings be doubled in all areas of their lives in Jesus' Name. Amen!

Wednesday, October 2nd

ONE-YEAR BIBLE PLAN: ISAIAH 46-48/ 2ND COR. 10:1-17

PREPARING FOR GROW 2/4

I. WHAT WE MUST DO AS A CONGREGATION:

B. ASSIMILATE AND NURTURE NEW MEMBERS: As great as our assemblies may be, they are only sometimes adequate. New members may remain "on the fringe."

New members may be left out of the "family life" of the congregation activities. If new members remain "on the fringe" for long, they may begin to look elsewhere, where they can be more involved and grow.

Babes in Christ often require special attention and nurturing. New Converts often bring with them many personal problems. They need the care of interested, mature Christians – Otherwise, they may soon "wither away." **Romans 15:1-3.**

What does it take for a congregation to provide such things? It begins with what we are willing to do individually. Each congregation can be stronger and more ready to grow than its members are willing to be.

> **Memory Verse: Romans 15:1-2:** *"We who are strong ought to bear with the scruples of the weak, and not to please ourselves. 2 Let each of us please his neighbor for his good, leading to edification."*

Thursday, October 3rd

ONE-YEAR BIBLE PLAN: ISAIAH 49-51/ 2ND COR. 11:1-16

Mark 1:2-3: *"... Behold, I send my messenger before thy face, Which shall prepare thy way before thee..."*

BE FAITHFUL

John the Baptist was the forerunner of Jesus Christ. He is to call people to repentance and believe in Him who should come. That was the core assignment of John the Baptist. He was called to point the people to the Lamb of God: **John 1:29.**

The ministry of John the Baptist wasn't glamorous. He was preaching in the wilderness, and his diet and mode of dressing reflected that: **Mark 1:6.** Nevertheless, Jesus said: *"Verily I say unto you, Among them that are born of women there hath not risen a greater than John the Baptist: ..."* **Matthew 11:11.**

When we compare ourselves with ourselves as ministers of the Gospel, people try to classify which ministry is bigger and which is not. It is only God who knows which one is bigger. It only depends on your assigned assignment. Once you are faithful to what you are called to do, you are big in the sight of God, and you will receive the same reward as somebody who conquered the whole world.

Your faithfulness to what you are called to do in God's reward system matters. **Matthew 25:21.** It doesn't matter whether you are seen, commended, or otherwise. What matters is how faithful you are. It is your faithfulness that the Lord rewards. *Be faithful in your God-given assignment.*

Friday, October 4th

ONE-YEAR BIBLE PLAN: ISAIAH 52-54/ 2ND COR. 11:17-33

John 8:12: *"Then spake Jesus again unto them, saying, I am the light of the world: he that followeth me shall not walk in darkness, but shall have the light of life."*

FOLLOW HIS LEADING

Those who follow the Spirit's leading are the sons and daughters of God. Gideon was a great and charismatic leader. As he sought to win a great victory for the Lord against the Midianites, he gave his people an instruction, *"Look on me, and do likewise: and behold, when I come to the outside of the camp, it shall be that as I do, so shall ye do." "When I blow a trumpet, I and all that are with me, then blow ye the trumpets on every side of the camp, and say, The sword of the LORD, and Gideon."* **Judges 7:17-18.**

When the soldiers in Gideon's army followed this lead, they won a great victory against their enemies -the Midianites. Jesus Christ tells us the same today: *"Follow my lead, beloved."* Jesus, by this, urges us to be like Him in thought, speech, and action as a matter of priority.

Christlikeness-transforming to the image of Christ must be our focus. In Acts of the Apostles, people looked at the disciples and said they had been with Jesus. It means that they were Christlike.

Let us now examine how Jesus wants believers to follow His lead.

The Lord asks believers to do the following:

- Love as He has loved **John 13:34.**
- Endure injustice as He did **1st Peter 2:20-21.**

- Deny ourselves as He did **John 16:24.**
- Serve one another as Jesus served us **John 13:14-15.**
- Be humble as He was **Matthew 11:29.**
- Obey as He obeyed **Philippians 2:5-8.**
- Walk as He walked **1st John 2:6.**

Apostle Paul is a shining example of a believer who obeyed this instruction to follow Christ's lead. He was undoubtedly an imitator of Christ. He also encouraged others to be imitators of God. He wrote, *"Follow me as follow Christ."*

Apostle Paul and other Bible characters who followed Christ's lead experienced fulfillment in life and ministry. *As you make Christlikeness your goal and follow Christ's lead and examples daily, your life will be an amazing success story, in Jesus' Name.*

Prayer:

Power to be like Jesus, come upon me, in Jesus' Name.

Saturday, October 5th

ONE-YEAR BIBLE PLAN: ISAIAH 55-57/ 2ND COR. 12:1-11

OCTOBER PRAYER FIRESTORM

Ezekiel 29:1-2: *"In the tenth year, in the tenth month, on the twelfth day of the month, the word of the Lord came to me...."*

FIRESTORM DELIVERANCE PRAYER

- *Lord, we thank You for bringing us safely to October.* **Psalm 103:1-4**
- *Lord, thank you for bringing us to this month's Deliverance Prayer Firestorm.*
- *We take authority over this month in the Name of Jesus.*
- *This month, we shall rejoice and be glad in it.*
- *I cover every day of this month with the Blood of Jesus*—**Revelation 12:11**
- *I cover all our journey this month with the Blood of Jesus.*
- *Blood of Jesus Fight for us this month.*
- *Everything shall work together for good for us this month.*
- *My blessings attached to this month will be released!*
- *This month, The crisis assigned against my family shall backfire.*
- *Spirit of getting and losing assigned against me this month, be crushed.*
- *October is the month of double grace, Lord; give us double favor this month.* **2nd Peter 1:2.**

- Every good thing locked up by the devil against us is released by fire.
- Altars of darkness erected to make me cry this month catch fire now.
- Powers of darkness monitoring my family receive blindness now.
- Enemies waiting to laugh at me this month, be confounded. **Psalms 35:4.**
- Powers speaking poverty and infirmities into my destiny, die by fire.
- Powers speaking poverty, stagnancy, and infirmities into my destiny, be scattered by fire.
- Father, protect my family and me from evil this month.
- Lord, help me to continually dwell and abide in Your secret place in Jesus' name. **Psalms 91:1-2.**
- Holy Spirit, deliver me from the yoke of poverty and infirmity. **Isaiah 10:27.**
- Lord Jesus, protect me and my loved ones wherever we go this month.
- Father, open windows of marvelous opportunities for me this month.
- Come to my rescue, O God, and recover all my stolen favor and glory.
- Father, continually renew the strength of Apostle Stevie Okauru.
- Thank God for the prayer answered!

First Sunday in October

ONE-YEAR BIBLE PLAN: ISAIAH 58-60/ 2ND COR. 12:12-21

PREPARING FOR GROW 3/4

II. WHAT WE MUST DO AS INDIVIDUALS:

A. STRENGTHEN OUR RELATIONSHIP WITH GOD: Others must see the blessings of walking with God in us and not simply knowing about the Lord! We can't share what we do not have. No matter how strong our relationship with God, we can always improve. Paul recognized this in his own life. **Acts 3:6, Philippians 3:12-15.**

We must always grow spiritually. Thus, we must continue to add to our faith virtue, to virtue knowledge. Much of this is accomplished through personal and daily devotions. And personal efforts must be accompanied by frequent assembling. **2nd Pet. 1:5-8, Ps. 1:1-3, Heb. 10:24-25.**

B. STRENGTHEN OUR RELATIONSHIP WITH ONE ANOTHER: Our love and unity is a powerful witness for Christ - **John 13:34-35; John 17:20-21.**

A strong network of Christians is essential to assimilate and nurture New Believers. No matter how strong our relationship is, we can always improve. **1st Thessalonians 4:9-10; 1st Peter 1:22.**

So, we must seek out opportunities to strengthen our bond with Christ. Regular attendance will also help. And so is hospitality. **Hebrews 10:24-25, 1st Peter 4:8-9.**

Memory Verse: 1st Peter 1:22: *"Since you have purified your souls in obeying the truth [a]through the Spirit in [b]sincere love of the brethren, love one another fervently with a pure heart."*

Monday, October 7th

ONE-YEAR BIBLE PLAN: ISAIAH 61-63/ 2ND COR. 13:1-14

Hebrews 5:12 AMP: *"For even though by this time you ought to be teaching others, you need someone to teach you the first principles of God's Word again. You have come to need milk, not solid food."*

GROW IN THE LORD

3rd John 1:2: *"Beloved, I wish above all things that thou mayest prosper and be in health, even as thy soul prospereth."* Christ expects you as a follower to grow and move from one level to another and eventually to a level where you will be so blessed in the things of the spirit that you will become a blessing to others by teaching them what you have learned.

When you refuse to improve spiritually, you become a spiritual baby who is naive and unskilled in God's Word and can't handle a meat diet. **2nd Peter 3:18**

But when you study and apply the truth of the Word in all your endeavors, you grow in wisdom, in the knowledge of Jesus Christ, the Messiah; you increase understanding and power. You become solidly grounded.

That is why **Colossians 2:6-7 MSG says,** *"My counsel for you is simple and straightforward: Just go ahead with what you've been given. You received Christ Jesus, the Master; now live Him. You're deeply rooted in Him. You're well-constructed upon Him. You know your way around the faith. Now, do what you've been taught. School's out; quit studying the subject and start living it!"* Start doing His Word and grow!

Prayer: *"Lord, give the grace to do Your Word in Jesus' Name!*

Tuesday, October 8th

ONE-YEAR BIBLE PLAN: ISAIAH 64-66/ GALATIANS 1:1-24

Deuteronomy 6:6-7: *"These commandments that I give you today are to be on your hearts. Impress them on your children. Talk about them when you sit at home, walk along the road, lie down, and get up."*

THE WORD LIFE

John C. Maxwell said, *"The strength of our faith is not determined by how loudly we proclaim it, but by how deeply we live it."* Let's embrace the timeless wisdom of scriptures, ensuring it isn't just known but lived.

God's Word isn't a mere compilation of historical records or poetic verses; it's a way of life, a beacon guiding us through every season. The commands aren't burdens but blessings designed to lead us to a life of joy and purpose.

Faith isn't a solitary journey. It's communal, meant to be shared, discussed, and passed down. Our homes should resonate with conversations about God's teachings, becoming places where faith is nurtured, and love is evident.

We are entrusted with molding the next generation, ensuring they know God's commands and have them etched on their hearts.

Meditate and ask yourself: Is my daily life a reflection of God's commandments? How can I make conversations about His Word more integral to my household?

Prayer: *"Lord, help me shape the spiritual journey of my family in the Name of Jesus Christ. Amen!*

Wednesday, October 9th

ONE-YEAR BIBLE PLAN: JEREMIAH 1-3/ GALATIANS 2:1-21

PREPARING FOR GROW 4/4

C. DEVELOP RELATIONSHIPS WITH THE LOST. The light must shine in the darkness to be of much value - **Matthew 5:14-16.**

If people are sick, those with the cure must be willing to be among them - **Matthew 9:10-13.**

The right example can prepare people to receive the Word – **1st Peter 3:1-2.**

Relationships with the lost can be the basis for continued relationships with them after they are saved. Developing relationships with the lost is an ongoing process. But if an effort to share the gospel is not well-received, we may need to move on - **Matthew 7:6.**

Just as Jesus could not stay in one place, we can't limit our outreach to just a few friends, relatives, and neighbors forever - **Luke 4:42-44.**

Therefore, we must always look for new relationships with the lost. Simple hospitality will go a long way, both offered and accepted - **Matthew 9:9-13.**

Matthew extended hospitality to his friends soon after Jesus called him: Jesus accepted the opportunity to eat and be with the lost.

Inviting the lost to our assemblies can be very profitable. It allows them to meet other Christians. With whom they may also develop relationships.

To be useful to the Master, an individual must prepare himself – **2nd Timothy 2:21-22.**

The same is true regarding churches: The Lord will use a congregation that has prepared itself just as the Lord was willing to provide an open door for the church in Philadelphia - **Revelation 3:8.**

As we have seen, we must prepare ourselves both as a congregation and as individuals.

But the onus rests mostly upon us as individuals. For a chain is no stronger than its weakest link.

If we as individuals fail to do our part, any effort by the congregation as a whole is greatly weakened, if not mortally wounded!

Do we want to grow?

As with the physical body, gradual decay and death are the only alternatives to growth.

Shall we be like the church at Laodicea or the church at Philadelphia?

The answer may be whether we are "Getting Ready to Grow"!

Memory Verse: Revelation 3:8: *"I know your works. See, I have set before you an open door, and no one can shut it, for you have a little strength, have kept My word, and have not denied My name."*

Thursday, October 10th

ONE-YEAR BIBLE PLAN: JEREMIAH 4-6/ GALATIANS 3:1-29

Ephesians 3:19: *"And to know the love of Christ, which passeth knowledge, that ye might be filled with all the fulness of God."*

ALIVE IN YOU

The Bible says, "...Christ in you the hope of glory." **Colossians 1:27.** Christ in you means God alive in and at work in you. **2nd Corinthians 5:19** says, "To wit, that God was in Christ, reconciling the world unto himself, not imputing their trespasses unto them; and hath committed unto us the word of reconciliation." God worked in Christ as He walked the streets in Bible days doing those mighty miracles.

Also, **Colossians 1:19** says, "For it pleased the Father that in him should all fulness dwell." When Jesus walked the earth, all divinity was at home in Him. He was God alive—walking and talking in a man's body. But that's not the end. The same God is in you now as He was in Christ. Hallelujah!

Having received the Holy Spirit, God lives in you now; you're His temple. Through you, He impacts your world. He brings sinners out of darkness into His marvelous light. You're His extension on the earth today. Remember His words, "I will dwell in them, and walk in them, and I will be their God, and they shall be my people." **2nd Corinthians 6:16.**

He's talking in you and walking in you today. Every time you minister to someone about Jesus, God is at work and alive in you and through you. You must be faithful and diligent in soul-winning because the Father expresses His love and righteousness through you. Hallelujah!

Friday, October 11th

ONE-YEAR BIBLE PLAN: JEREMIAH 7-9/ GALATIANS 4:1-31

Matthew 26:33: *"Peter answered and said unto him, Though all men shall be offended because of thee, yet will I never be offended."*

IN GOD

Like Peter, we are often more confident in ourselves than in God. And then we are devastated when we fail because we think we are infallible.

We must realize that our flesh is just as capable of sin as anyone else's. If we fall, it should concern us but not surprise us. We should realize with Paul that *'in my flesh dwelleth no good thing,'* get back into the spirit through confession and forgiveness, and get on with Jesus.

The Lord has never had anyone qualified to work for Him. Peter wasn't qualified, and we were neither at our best. If we realize that we are nothing and have nothing, then we are prime candidates to be used by God. Peter became the best-known of the twelve apostles. The Lord used him mightily. But He didn't want him, or us, to forget that it was Christ in Peter and not Peter himself who was great.

This also illustrates the extent of our Father's love and forgiveness. If God forgave Peter for his sin and reinstated and advanced him, then we have not pushed God's grace beyond its limit. Where sin abounds, grace abounds much more. God doesn't see us as a failure – just learners. God can redeem the worst 'failure' and work it together for good **Romans 8:28.** Let's think like God.

Saturday, October 12th

ONE-YEAR BIBLE PLAN: JEREMIAH 10-12/ GALATIANS 5:1-26

WISDOM OF THE ORACLE

LEADERSHIP BY SERVANTHOOD

- Those who go through the school of servanthood and stewardship graduate into leadership.
- Only when servanthood and stewardship are accredited will leadership be certified.
- A leadership cap fits only a servant's head.
- Only those who stoop to serve will ever rise to lead.
- You first take a servant's position; then, God will give you leadership.
- Jesus became a servant before God gave Him a highly exalted leadership position.
- Serve today committedly to lead tomorrow successfully.

Second Sunday in October

ONE-YEAR BIBLE PLAN: JEREMIAH 13-15/ GALATIANS 6:1-18

DIVINE SIGNPOSTS 1/5

To lead people to Christ, we must understand the importance of the Word of God - **Romans 10:17.**

The gospel is the power of God to salvation - **Romans 1:16.**

But we must also complement the Word by demonstrating certain qualities whereby people can see the gospel's truth in action. **John 13:34-35; John 15:12.**

People are more likely to believe in Jesus Christ when we demonstrate Christlikeness.

These 'signposts' can serve to let the nonbeliever know:

1. That there is a God Who loves them. A God who sent Jesus as a manifestation of that love.

2. These signposts let the true searcher know: those who are true disciples of Christ, who can thus lead them to Christ.

There are at least four such "Divine Signposts":

I. THE SIGNPOST OF UNITY:

A. THE VALUE OF UNITY OF BELIEVERS: God has sent Christ - **John 17:21.**

It shows that God loved the world - **John 17:23.**

> **Memory Verse: John 17:21:** *"That they all may be one, as You, Father, are in Me, and I in You; that they also may be one in Us, that the world may believe that You sent Me."*

Monday, October 14th

ONE-YEAR BIBLE PLAN: JEREMIAH 16-18/ EPHES. 1:1-23

2nd Kings 22:11-20: *"…therefore, my wrath shall be kindled against this place, and shall not be quenched."*

I Prophesy the Lord's judgment over you is forestalled!

"….. and thine eyes shall not see all the evil I will bring upon this place. And they brought the king word again." **[Verse 18-20]**. Until the death of King Josiah, the judgment of death that God passed on Israel was suspended. King Josiah's previous action triggered that postponement; on hearing that the judgment of God had been passed on Israel because of the sins of his fathers, he went to God in prayers, interceding for the people with supplications. For that reason, God decided to avert the calamity.

Many have the judgment of God awaiting them even before they are born. This is because of the sins of their forefathers, which have built evil foundations for them. These faulty foundations cause evil occurrences and misfortunes in their lives. And until these shaky foundations of sin are repaired, people always have calamity as their identity.

Are you one of these people? Have you been marked for destruction because of the iniquities of your forefathers? *Today, in the Name of Jesus, I intercede to God on your behalf for mercy. The mercy of God shall fall on you in Jesus' Name. Amen!*

Prayer:

Lord, I plead for mercy for me and my children to deliver us from the judgment in Jesus' Name. Amen!

Tuesday, October 15th

ONE-YEAR BIBLE PLAN: JEREMIAH 19-21/ EPHES. 2:1-22

James 1:6-8: *"He that wavereth is like a wave of the sea driven with the wind and tossed. Let not that man think that he shall receive anything from the Lord. A double-minded man is unstable in all his ways."*

HESITATE NOT

What happens when you hesitate to do something God told you to do? Your adversary takes the first step. The devil gets the jump on you.

If you want to live by faith, hesitation is one of the most hazardous habits you could ever have. It comes from needing more time to decide. The Bible says such a man is *"Unstable and unreliable and uncertain about everything he thinks, feels, decides."* If you are double-minded, the decisions you make are split. You try to live by faith and protect your fear simultaneously. You make faith statements like *"I believe God is going to heal me."* Then your fear whispers, *"But I wouldn't want to say I'm well just yet."* You're so busy going back and forth between faith and fear that you can't progress.

Kick the habit of hesitation today. Make a solid decision to trust in and act on the Word of God. Settle it forever. Resolve never to entertain doubts again. When doubt comes to your mind, cast it out quickly. When God speaks, don't waste a moment. Step right out in faith. That way, you can always keep the devil a step behind you!

Prayer: *I shall not hesitate at the Word of God!*

Wednesday, October 16th

ONE-YEAR BIBLE PLAN: JEREMIAH 22-24/ EPHES. 3:1-21

DIVINE SIGNPOSTS 2/5

THE SIGNPOST OF UNITY:

B. SO UNITY IS A SIGNPOST TO THE WORLD: to prove that God loves the world - **John 3:16.**

That God sent Christ who produces the unity witnessed by the world - **Ephesians 2:13-16.**

C. THE IMPORTANCE OF UNITY: Led Paul to condemn division and those who cause it – **1st Corinthians 1:10; Romans 16:17-18.**

The importance of unity also led Paul to teach attitudes essential to preserving unity - **Ephesians 4:1-3** and **Philippians 2:2-4.**

So, let's be sure that we do nothing to destroy the 'signpost' of unity; rather, let's work toward enhancing its effectiveness.

Another 'signpost' that points people in the right direction is The signpost of love, our next study topic.

Memory Verse: Philippians 2:2-4: *"Fulfill my joy by being like-minded, having the same love, being of one accord of one mind. 3 Let nothing be done through selfish ambition or conceit, but in lowliness of mind let each esteem others better than himself. 4 Let each of you look out not only for his interests but also for the interests of others."*

Thursday, October 17th

ONE-YEAR BIBLE PLAN: JEREMIAH 25-26/ EPHES. 4:1-32

Isaiah 40:31: *"But those who hope in the Lord will renew their strength. They will soar on wings like eagles...."*

RENEWED STRENGTH

Charles Spurgeon said, "It's not the strength of your faith that saves you, but the strength of Him upon whom you rely."

At times, the weight of the world might seem too much. Moments may arise when hope seems distant and strength feels depleted. But isn't it beautiful that God whispers the loudest in these moments?

Isaiah's words are more than just a promise; they are a divine assurance. They remind us that our strength doesn't come from our abilities but from our hope in the Lord. When we turn to Him, we don't just find strength; we find wings to rise, stamina to run our race, and the grace to journey ahead without growing faint.

So, in this moment, no matter where you find yourself, let the depth of God's promise sink in. When weariness creeps in, when the journey feels long, hope in the Lord. He's ready to renew, refresh, and rejuvenate your spirit.

Are you allowing the world's weight to pull you down? Or you are drawing on God's strength to rise above life's challenges.

Prayer:

Lord, empower to rise on grace and strength in the Name of Jesus, Chris. Amen!

Friday, October 18th

ONE-YEAR BIBLE PLAN: JEREMIAH 27/ EPHESIANS 5:1-16

2nd Corinthians 2:14 ESV: *"But thanks be to God, who in Christ always leads us in triumphal procession, and through us spreads the fragrance of the knowledge of him everywhere."*

VICTORY ON THE WAY

Are you facing challenges or difficulties today? Something could easily discourage you and cause you to give up on your dreams. I want to remind you that where you are differs from where you will stay. God has a good plan in store for your future. You'll walk right into victory when you stay in step with Him. The Scripture tells us that God wants to take us from glory to glory, from victory to victory. Even if you are between victories right now, keep your passion. Keep your enthusiasm. Focus on the fact that God has another level for you—another level of glory, another level of increase, another level of His favor.

Today, I encourage you to go out with a smile. Give Him your best. When you thank God for what He has done, you are sowing a seed that He will use in your future. Keep praying, believing, hoping, and standing strong because another victory is coming your way!

Prayer:

Father, As I focus my mind and heart completely on You. Help me step out of discouragement, out of complacency, out of worry, and into Your glory in Jesus' Name. Amen.

Saturday, October 19th

ONE-YEAR BIBLE PLAN: JEREMIAH 28/ EPHESIANS 5:2-33

WISDOM OF THE ORACLE

DEFINITION AND DIRECTION

- A clear definition will birth a strong direction to destiny.
- Where life ceases to follow a clear definition, it will suffer deviation that will result in derailment.
- Keep redefining your mission in life.
- Cross-check and re-appraise the direction you are following from time to time.
- Be sensitive! One degree, of course, can spell doom if you are not quickly redirected.

Third Sunday in October

ONE-YEAR BIBLE PLAN: JEREMIAH 31-32/ PHILIPP. 1:1-29

DIVINE SIGNPOSTS 3/5

II. THE SIGNPOST OF LOVE:

A. LOVE FOR ONE ANOTHER: shows that we have been loved by Christ, whose love we seek to emulate - **John 13:34.**

It shows that we are truly His disciples - **John 13:35.**

B. SO LOVE IS A SIGNPOST TO THE WORLD: and proves that Christ has loved us - **John 15:12-13.**

It also shows that those who emulate His love are His true disciples - **Ephesians 5:1-2.**

C. THE IMPORTANCE OF LOVE: Caused Paul encouraged churches to increase in love – **1st Thess. 4:9-10.**

The importance of love also led Paul to consider love as the "bond of perfection" - **Colossians 3:14.**

Here, we see that love and unity go together. Our love for one another makes us more likely to preserve our unity in Christ.

Unity and love also go hand in hand as "Divine Signposts." Unity lets people know God loves them, and love shows people who are the true followers of Christ. And we must also know faith does not work without love. **Galatians 5:6; 1st Corinthians 13:2.**

Memory Verse: Colossians 3:14: *"But above all these things put on love, which is the bond of perfection."*

Monday, October 21st

ONE-YEAR BIBLE PLAN: JEREMIAH 33-34/ PHILIPP. 2:1-30

Ezekiel 18:30-32: *".... so, iniquity shall not be your ruin. Cast away from you all your transgressions..."*

CONFESS FAITH WORD

The Bible says out of the abundance of the heart, the mouth speaks, so when you are prophesying to yourself, you are prophesying in faith, but the Bible says faith without works is dead. It is not enough to say, I will prosper and then do nothing! You have to back what you say with action.

David said, Goliath, you are dead. Then he ran to battle. So, Saint, whatever you do from now on, do it quickly. Stop being slothful; if you are going to reach the top, you don't drag your feet! Seest thou a man diligent in his business? He will stand before kings, saith the Lord in His word.

PRAYER:

Call on the Almighty God to save your souls; tell Him to be merciful. Father, forgive all my sins. Lord Jesus, come into my life. I surrender my life to you. If you forgive me my sins, Lord, I will serve You all the days of my life. Please have mercy on me. Thank You! Because You promised that whosoever will come to You, You will in no wise cast out. Father, I have come now. Receive me in Jesus' Name!

Forgive me and save my soul in Jesus' Name! Cleanse me in Your blood and write my name in the Book of Life, and I will serve You for the rest of my life. From now on, Lord, answer me in Jesus' Name anytime I call on you! Thank You, Father! In Jesus' mighty Name, I have prayed. Amen!

Tuesday, October 22nd

ONE-YEAR BIBLE PLAN: JEREMIAH 35-36/ PHILIPP. 3:1-21

Romans 5:3–5: *"...tribulation worketh patience; and patience, experience; and experience, hope; and hope maketh not ashamed..."*

VICTORY OVER TEMPTATION

God never promised to remove temptation from us, for even Christ was subject to it. The Bible says, *"He was tested in all things, like as we, yet without sin."*

There is no good reason to seek to escape, for such testing times have beneficial effects. There is a sense of achievement and assurance that results from victory over temptation that cannot come to us otherwise.

Temptation shows what people are. It does not make us Christian or un-Christian. It makes the Christian stronger and causes him to discover powerful resources.

You can benefit from what might be a tragedy if you only discover that in a time of temptation. Christ can become more real to you than ever, and His salvation will become more meaningful during tribulation. Be strong in the Lord and the power of His might. Amen!

Prayer:

In all times of temptation, may I remember Your example, Lord Jesus. Amen!

Wednesday, October 23rd

ONE-YEAR BIBLE PLAN: JEREMIAH 37-38/ PHILIPP. 4:1-23

DIVINE SIGNPOSTS 4/5

III. THE SIGNPOST OF HOPE

A. WHAT IS THE VALUE OF HOPE AS A DIVINE SIGNPOST?
Hope can prompt people to ask us questions. It helps us to share the reason for our hope **1st Peter 3:15.**

B. SO, HOPE IS A SIGNPOST TO THE WORLD: If our hope is noticeable, it will prompt people to ask, **"Why?"** Based upon reason, i.e., evidence for our faith, especially when our hope is through faith. **Hebrews 11:1.**

Hope accompanied by peace and joy – **Rom. 5:1-2**
Hope that is steadfast in tribulation - **Rom. 5:3-4**
Hope that is based on the love of God - **Romans 5:5.**
Hope assured by Christ's resurrection. **1st Peter 1:3.**

C. HOPE: It is so important that it led Peter to command Christians to set their hope fully on the grace to come – **1st Peter 1:13.**

Hope led Peter to command Christians always to be ready to explain their hope – **1st Peter 3:15.**

Add unity, love, and hope as "Divine Signposts." We will consider a final 'signpost.' In the next lesson.

Memory Verse: Romans 5:5: *"Now hope does not disappoint, because the love of God has been poured out in our hearts by the Holy Spirit who was given to us."*

Thursday, October 24th

ONE-YEAR BIBLE PLAN: JEREMIAH 39-40/ COL. 1:1-29

Philippians 2:14-15: *"Do all things without murmurings and disputing: That ye may be blameless and harmless, the sons of God, without rebuke, in a crooked and perverse nation, among whom ye shine as lights in the world."*

THE LIGHT

There's so much poverty in the world that's not supposed to be. Poverty is not from God; it's artificial; it is darkness. Poverty results from the selfishness of man, and that's because Satan introduced that selfishness into man's heart.

He's responsible for the darkness in our world. But thanks be unto God! The Bible says even though darkness shall cover the earth and gross darkness the people, we're to arise and shine **Isaiah 60:2-3.** God sent the Church of Jesus Christ as a light to the nations. And in these last days, we'll shine with maximum intensity.

This is the time for us, as God's people, to use what God has given us and take our place as the world's light. The Bible says, *"...the dark places of the earth are full of the habitations of cruelty."* **Psalm 74:20.**

But when we take our place, no force, adversary, or adversity on earth can withstand us. So, arise and shine. Impact your world. You're the hope and solution that the world needs. The Lord has sent you to bring glory, excellence, and meaning to the lives of those around you. You're His hands of love, mercy, and compassion to your world. Hallelujah!

Friday, October 25th

ONE-YEAR BIBLE PLAN: JER. 41-42/ COLOSSIANS 2:1-23

Psalm 121:1-2: *"I will lift my eyes to the hills—From whence comes my help? 2 My help comes from the Lord, Who made heaven and earth."*

WHERE HELP IS

In our daily walk, it's not uncommon to feel overwhelmed by life's 'mountains'—obstacles that seem too steep, too formidable. Yet, nestled within **Psalm 121:1-2** lies a profound invitation: to lift our eyes beyond these daunting heights to the Maker of heaven and earth. It's a gentle yet powerful reminder that our help comes from the Lord, not the towering challenges or the rugged terrains we encounter.

The mountains that intimidate us can also lead us to seek God's presence more earnestly. They remind us that our true strength doesn't lie in our ability to climb or conquer but in the unshakeable support of the One who created all things. This realization doesn't mean the mountains disappear, but it changes how we approach them. We climb not in isolation but accompanied by the Creator, who knows every crevice and peak.

As we face our mountains today, let's remember this: they are not just obstacles but signposts pointing you toward a deeper dependence on God. No matter how strenuous, each step upward gets you closer to Him. Today, remember that your help comes from the Lord, who watches over and protects you. Trust in Him and rely on His unfailing love and faithfulness.

Saturday, October 26th

ONE-YEAR BIBLE PLAN: JER. 43-44/ COLOSSIANS 3:1-2

WISDOM OF THE ORACLE

NEVER ASSUME PROGRESS

- It would be best if you refrained from assuming progress to make progress.
- Just like a vehicle will never assume motion unless it is engaged.
- It is the engagement of things that birth progress.
- The real progressives don't discuss progress; they engage to make progress.
- They don't stop at the line of thought; they line up action steps.
- They don't stop at the school of thought; they graduate into the school of action.
- They are not mere philosophers; they graduate to become explorers and adventurers.

Fourth Sunday in October

ONE-YEAR BIBLE PLAN: JER. 45-46/ COLOSSIANS 4:1-18

DIVINE SIGNPOSTS 5/5

IV. THE SIGNPOST OF GOOD WORKS:

A. GOOD WORKS IS OF UTMOST VALUE AS A DIVINE SIGNPOST: Good work leads people to glorify our Father in heaven - **Matthew 5:16.**

Good works lead people to glorify God on the day of visitation – **1ˢᵗ Peter 2:12.**

B. GOOD WORKS IS A SIGNPOST TO THE WORLD: It directs people to consider the motivation behind such works. Good works open people up to the gospel, which inspires such works – **1ˢᵗ Peter 3:1-2.**

C. THE IMPORTANCE OF GOOD WORKS: Led Paul to command that we be ready for every good work. It also led Paul to command that we maintain good works. **Titus 3:1; Titus 3:8; Titus 3:14.**

In conclusion, with these "Divine Signposts," we can see how people can be led to Christ:

1. Our unity can convince people of God's love for them in sending Christ.

2. Our love can direct them to true disciples of Christ.

3. Our hope can prompt them to ask questions about our faith's reason.

4. Our good works can encourage them to glorify God by obeying the gospel.

This in no way takes away from the power of the gospel to save souls. But the Lord intended His church to be a city on a hill. Demonstrating certain qualities as a group would draw people to Him.

Without these "Divine Signposts," we make it much harder for souls searching for their Savior and His gospel!

Are we partaking in the local congregation to display unity, love, hope, and good works?

Memory Verse: Titus 3:14: *"And let our people also learn to maintain good works, to meet urgent needs, that they may not be unfruitful."*

Monday, October 28th

ONE-YEAR BIBLE PLAN: JER. 47-48/1ST THESS. CHAP. 1&2

1st Corinthians 15:10: *"But by the grace of God, I am what I am: and his grace which was bestowed upon me was not in vain; but I labored more abundantly than they all: yet not I but the grace of God which was with me."*

GOD'S GRACE

Grace is the reason Christ went to Calvary. Grace covers our errors and colors our efforts. God's grace is the distinguishing factor in people's lives. The difference between the two believers is the dimension of grace they access.

There are diverse levels of grace. There is grace; there is a great grace; there is exceeding grace and multiplied grace. That is why we must grow in grace **2nd Peter 3:18.** Your present level of grace can increase.

The difference between Paul and the other apostles was grace. He said by the grace of God, I am what I am. It means, 'If you like my results, what you need is the level of grace in which I operate.'

The acronym for G-R-A-C-E is God's Riches At Christ's Expense. God sacrificed Christ for His riches to be available to us. **Romans 5:8; 2nd Corinthians 8:9.**

Grace is God's seal of approval and acceptance. To access God's grace, live a humble life. **James 4:6, 1st Peter 5:5, Proverbs 3:34.** You activate God's grace at the prayer altar. So, ask God to grant you the spirit of supplication.

Prayer: *Lord, Multiply your grace in my life!*

Tuesday, October 29th

ONE-YEAR BIBLE PLAN: JER. 49-50/1ST THESS. CHAP. 3&4

John 13:20: *"Verily, verily, I say unto you, He that receiveth whomsoever I send receiveth me, and he that receiveth me receiveth him that sent me."*

RECEIVE GOD'S SERVANT

I can't tell you how many born-again, Holy Ghost-filled Believers pick their pastor apart on Saturday night and then expect him to pray the prayer of faith for them on Sunday morning! They'll constantly make critical comments about the evangelists and preachers that God has sent to minister to them and then wonder why the rain of the Spirit has all but dried up in their lives.

Most of those folks would never dream of criticizing the ministry of Jesus. Yet, according to the Word of God, that's precisely what they're doing. Jesus said, *"He that receiveth whomsoever I send receiveth me."*

I know ministers fail sometimes. I know they make mistakes. Jesus knew they would, too. But, even so, He said, *"If you receive them, you receive Me."*

If you think some preacher's doctrine is wrong, pray for him. Stop sitting under his ministry if necessary. But the Scripture says, *"Who are you to judge someone else's servant? To his own master, he stands or falls. And he will stand, for the Lord can make him stand."* **Romans 14:4 NIV.**

Prayer: *"Lord, deliver me from being judgmental of your minister in the name of Jesus Christ. Amen!*

Wednesday, October 30th

ONE-YEAR BIBLE PLAN: JEREMIAH 51-52/1ST THESS. 5:1-28

EXAMPLES WORTH FOLLOWING 1/5

The Bible speaks of examples: Imitating those who are good examples – **1st Cori. 11:1; Philippians 3:17; Hebrews 13:7.**

Apart from following godly example, we must also be a good example to others – **1st Timothy 4:12.**

1. Who is my example and role model as a Christian?

2. Whose example am I as a Christian?

3. Who does my life and my character influence?

3. What kind of example do I set as a Christian?

In this study, "Examples Worth Following," we shall consider these questions more carefully.

I. WHO IS YOUR EXAMPLE?

A. IS IT THE LORD JESUS CHRIST? Jesus was the example of Apostle Paul – **1st Corinthians 11:1 NIV.**

Jesus should be our example as well:

#1. On how to please one another. **Romans 15:1-3 TLB; NIV.** #2. On how to love one another. **Ephesians 5:1-2 TLB; MSG.** #3. On how to look out for one another - **Philippians 2:4-5.** #4. How to suffer patiently when mistreated. **1st Pet. 2:20-23.**

Jesus is our prime example in all the above situations!

> **Memory Verse: 1st Peter 2:21:** *"For to this you were called, because Christ also suffered for us, leaving us an example, that you should follow His steps."*

Thursday, October 31st

ONE-YEAR BIBLE PLAN: LAM. 1-3/2ND THESS. 1&2

Exodus 15:26: *"... I will put none of these diseases upon thee, which I have brought upon the Egyptians: for I am the Lord that healeth thee."*

HEALTH FOR YOU

Has the devil ever tried to condemn you by telling you that it's contrary to the principles of faith to use doctors and medicine when you need healing? If so, know now that it is God's will to heal you. If your faith is strong and you can believe the Word without wavering, regardless of your symptoms, then you can receive that healing by faith alone.

But that kind of faith takes more than just hearing a few sermons about healing. It takes a deep personal revelation of God's healing power. So, if you haven't yet developed that kind of faith, the doctor is your best friend. If you're not certain whether your faith is strong enough or whether you need a doctor's help, follow the instructions of Paul in **Colossians 3:15.** And let peace be your umpire.

If fear rises within you when you think about doing without medical help, then go to a doctor. And go in faith! On the other hand, if you have confidence that healing is yours strictly by faith, let your faith do its work and receive your healing directly. Whether or not you go to the doctor is not the issue. It is what you do with your faith. Either way, you can rejoice knowing God is working with you, meeting you at the level of your faith. Thank God for your healing—however it comes! Do not let Satan condemn you. It is none of his business!

Friday, November 1st

ONE-YEAR BIBLE PLAN: LAM. 4-5/2ND THESS. 3:1-18

Psalm 47:4-7: "*.... Sing praises: sing praises unto our King. God is the King of all the earth: sing ye praises with understanding.*"

PRAISE GOD

Praise releases the Holy Spirit into every area of our lives. As you praise Him, you offer thanksgiving for His mercy, grace, goodness, power, healing, love, favor, and blessings. Praise the Lord now!

PRAISE THE LORD NOW

You are the Lord of Hosts, the I AM THAT I AM, the Rock of Ages, the Unchangeable Lord, the Ancient of Days. I Magnify Your Holy Name! Your Name is Wonderful, Counselor! Mighty God! The Everlasting Father! The Prince of Peace! You are the Lion of the Tribe of Judah! You are worthy of being praised and worshipped in Jesus' name. Amen!

BIRTHDAY AND ANNIVERSARY PRAYERS

Father, I commit all your November children and those celebrating an anniversary this month unto you. Lord, as they begin a New Year, replace everything old with something new. Give them new joy, new blessings, and breakthroughs. Let everything become new in all areas of their lives, and let them serve you to the very end, in Jesus' Name. Amen!

Saturday, November 2nd

ONE-YEAR BIBLE PLAN: EZEKIEL 1-3/1ST TIMOTHY 1:1-20

NOVEMBER PRAYER FIRESTORM

Deuteronomy 1:3: *"And it came to pass in the fortieth year, in the eleventh month, on the first [day] of the month, [that] Moses spake unto the children of Israel, according unto all that the LORD had given him in commandment unto them."*

FIRESTORM DELIVERANCE PRAYER

- Father, thank bringing me to the November Deliverance Prayer Firestorm!
- Thank You, Lord, for protection and preservation.
- Thank you for the power in the Blood of Jesus that can deliver to the utmost!
- Thank You, for no power can challenge Your power.
- Thank You, the firepower of the Holy Ghost.
- Thank You, Lord, for this month, You shall restore all we have lost.
- Lord, in this month of restoration, restore all that I have lost.
- Father, this month, burn every garment of poverty and infirmity in my life.
- This month, I will receive an increase in my prosperity.
- O God, Arise and permanently disgrace all my problems with divine solutions.

- O God, arise and scatter every power saying no to the growth of this Ministry.
- Father, we repent of the sins that opened the door to pestilence in our lives in the Name of Jesus.
- O Lord, let Your mercy speak for us this month.
- Divine immunity overshadows our health workers by the Blood of Jesus.
- Lord, thank You for the benefits of the Blood of Jesus.
- Troublers of the Israel of this Ministries, the God of Elijah, and Elisha to trouble you.
- Demons fighting the dedication of church members be bound in the Name of Jesus Christ.
- Holy Spirit, Baptize me with your fire and power today!
- The blood of Jesus envelopes me and my family now.
- I overcome every spirit of infirmity by the blood of the Lamb, in Jesus' Name.
- The blood of Jesus speaks confusion into the enemy's camp, in Jesus' Name.
- Blood of Jesus minister defeats every evil work in my life in Jesus' Name.
- I bind and cast out all spirits of fear in Jesus' Name.
- Father, let the power of salvation overshadow our nations.
- The tongue of discouragement against this church, be silenced!

○   *Wicked mouth assigned to stop us be crushed now!*

First Sunday in November

ONE-YEAR BIBLE PLAN: EZEKIEL 4-5/1ˢᵀ TIM. CH. 2&3

EXAMPLES WORTH FOLLOWING 2/5

B. IS IT THE APOSTLE PAUL?

1. He urged the Corinthians – **1ˢᵗ Corinthians 4:6; 1ˢᵗ Corinthians 11:1 AMPC.**
2. To give no offense – **1ˢᵗ Corinthians 10:32.**
3. To seek the benefit of others – **1ˢᵗ Cor. 10:33 TLB.**
4. As he urged the Philippians - **Philippians 3:17.**
5. To not consider themselves as having attained perfection - **Philippians 3:12.**
6. To press on to maturity - **Philippians 3:12-15.**
7. To live according to the level that we have learned - **Philippians 3:16.**
8. To enjoy a close relationship with the God of peace - **Philippians 4:9.**
9. **To receive and do the word even in affliction.** And praise and encourage others to do the same as Paul praised and encouraged the Thessalonians: For receiving the Word despite affliction – **1ˢᵗ Thessalonians 1:6.**
10. **We are to avoid being a burden to others** – **2ⁿᵈ Thessalonians 3:7-10.**

Paul and other New Testament Christians provide wonderful examples for us to follow.

Memory Verse: 1ˢᵗ Thessalonians 1:6.

Monday, November 4th

ONE-YEAR BIBLE PLAN: EZEKIEL 6-7/1ST TIM. CH. 4-5

James 1:21-22 GWT: "…… *This word can save you. Do what God's Word says. Don't merely listen to it.…*"

DO THE WORD

Isaiah 60:1-3 says arise and shine. Arise means get up, spring into action, and start putting what you know to work. But what you know alone will not give you your breakthrough. You also need to apply what you know to receive your desired result. Wisdom is the correct application of knowledge.

Nothing happens except somebody makes it happen, or put in another way, nothing works except somebody works it. No matter how great, your talent will only be useful if you use it. You will not get anything from God if you are a hearer only and not a doer of the Word. If He says give and you shall be given, and you refuse to give, you will not receive. And if you expect to receive without giving, you deceive yourself.

If the Lord says pay your tithes, and He will open the windows of Heaven over you and pour out a blessing for you that your storage cannot contain the blessing, but you say I don't care. He will close His Heavens as you retain your tithe. And things will continue to be tight for you. Today, I pray for you to grant *me the wisdom, and grace to be doer of God's Word in Jesus' Name. Amen!*

Prayer: *Lord, give the grace always to do Your Word in the Name of Jesus Christ. Amen!*

Tuesday, November 5th

ONE-YEAR BIBLE PLAN: EZEKIEL 8-9/1ST TIMOTHY 6:1-21

Galatians 5:6: *"For in Christ Jesus neither circumcision nor uncircumcision has any value. The only thing that counts is faith expressing itself through love."*

LOVE AND FAITH

"To one who has faith, no explanation is necessary. To one without faith, no explanation is possible." **Thomas Aquinas.**

As you read this, may it remind you of God's ever-present love in your path today. May each step you take today be steps of faith, walking hand in hand with your Savior.

In **Galatians 5:6,** Paul reminds us of an essential truth: the heart matters most to God. It's not about outward symbols or traditions but our inner conviction and how we let that faith manifest through love. This faith-love synergy is the heartbeat of a genuine Christian life. It's about letting our inner beliefs manifest in loving actions, making our faith tangible.

Meditate on how you can authentically live out your faith today. Does your faith find its truest expression in acts of love towards those around you? Think about it! Act on it!

Prayer:

Lord Jesus, Thank you for the gift of faith and the command to love. Teach me to live in a way that my faith is always visible through my love. May every act, every word, every thought be infused with the love that stems from genuine faith in You. In Jesus' Name, I pray, Amen.

Wednesday, November 6th

ONE-YEAR BIBLE PLAN: EZEKIEL 10-12/2ND TIM. CH. 1&2

EXAMPLES WORTH FOLLOWING 3/5

C. IS IT OTHER FAITHFUL CHRISTIANS? As Paul encouraged the Philippians in - **Philippians 3:17.**

- a) **To note those walking like Paul** and to consider them a pattern to follow.

- b) **To imitate the faith and patience** of those who inherit the promises - **Hebrews 6:12.**

- c) **To follow the faith** of those who rule over us - **Hebrews 13:7.**

Many Christians today provide examples worthy of emulation:

Whose example are you following? We are either imitating either Christ or some other Christian, either living or dead.

Does your life suggest that your example is less than exemplary like the Laodiceans - **Revelation 3:14-16?**

Closely related to this question of whose example we follow is, is another question we shall tackle in our next lesson:

Memory Verse: Hebrews 13:7: *"Remember those who rule over you, who have spoken the word of God to you, whose faith follow, considering the outcome of their conduct."*

Thursday, November 7th

ONE-YEAR BIBLE PLAN: EZEKIEL 13-14/2ND TIM. CH. 3&4

Philippians 3:10: *"That I may know him, and the power of his resurrection, and the fellowship of his sufferings, being made conformable unto his death."*

THE DEEP CALLETH 1/2

Philippians 3:10 is one of the deepest passages in the Scriptures. Paul wrote practically two-thirds of the New Testament. This man suffered for Christ. He did not marry. He spent his life preaching the gospel. He was eventually crucified and persecuted.

He said, *"That I may know Him..."* He was taken to paradise three times and still prayed the prayer point: *"I may know Him..."*

One of the major spiritual problems of our days is being superficial and shallow. There is a preponderance of many superficial, surface-life, and very shallow Christians. The truth is that in the last few days, the situation will get worse. People will get more superficial. If we are deep, the way God wants us to be deep, we should speak terror into the enemy's camp, and they would beg us to spare them.

Prayer:

1. *God, arise, break, and remold me, in Jesus' Name.*
2. *Hand of the wicked holding my glory and shining, I cut you off, in the name of Jesus.*
3. *Every wicked altar chanting my name catches fire.*
4. *Powers mocking God in my life; your time is up.*

Friday, November 8th

ONE-YEAR BIBLE PLAN: EZEKIEL 15-16/ TITUS 1:1-16

Philippians 3:10: *"That I may know him, and the power of his resurrection, and the fellowship of his sufferings, being made conformable unto his death."*

THE DEEP CALLETH 2/2

Deep calleth unto deep. Surface calleth unto the surface. Height calleth unto height. It is a divine principle. It does not change.

Deep people have experienced new birth, Biblical salvation, and genuine sanctification. And are filled with the Holy Spirit. They have also received the baptism of the Holy Ghost with the evidence of speaking in tongues and are filled with the Word of God. They are prayer addicts and intercessors.

Beloved, I encourage you to learn from the lives of Jesus Christ and Apostle Paul and imitate them. You will grow more spiritually in the Lord.

Also, begin to win souls. God loves soul winners, and He will get more intimate with you. Beloved, pay the price, and become a deep Christian today.

Prayer:

1. Ancient satanic powers, release me, in Jesus' Name.
2. Dark robbers hear the word of the Lord; release me by fire.
3. O God, arise, reposition me for signs and wonders.
4. Thank You, Lord, For answering my prayers in the Name of Jesus Christ. Amen!

Saturday, November 9th

ONE-YEAR BIBLE PLAN: EZEKIEL 17-18/ TITUS CH. 2&3

WISDOM OF THE ORACLE

WISDOM MATTERS

- Wisdom is the Master Key to the Treasures of Life.

- That is why God told Solomon, *"Because this was in thine heart, and thou hast not asked riches, wealth, or honor, nor the life of thine enemies, neither yet hast asked long life...Wisdom and knowledge are granted unto thee, and I will give thee riches, and wealth, and honor, such as none of the kings have had that have been before thee."* **2nd Chronicles 1:11-12.**

- Wisdom is better than jewels or money **Proverbs 8:11.**

- Wisdom guarantees promotion **Proverbs 4:8.**

- Wisdom brings you favor and recognition **Proverbs 8:35.**

- Seek wisdom!

Second Sunday in November

ONE-YEAR BIBLE PLAN: EZEKIEL 19-20/ PHILEMON CH. 1

EXAMPLES WORTH FOLLOWING 4/5

II. WHOSE EXAMPLE ARE YOU?

A. IS IT OTHER CHRISTIANS?

1. Your brothers and sisters in the Lord?

2. Especially those who are babes in Christ?

3. Or even older Christians?

We should be mindful of the example we are to one another. – **1ˢᵗ Thessalonians 1:7; 1ˢᵗ Timothy 4:12; Titus 2:7.**

B. IS IT YOUNG CHILDREN? *1. Who naturally looks up to their parents? 2. Who is also influenced by others?*

Adults like their parents. Older children as well. Christians should be mindful of their example to the young. **Mat. 18:6.**

C. IS IT UNBELIEVERS? *1. Who sees if we "walk the talk"? 2. Who often gauges the value of following Christ by our example? 3. Who judges the church by its members?*

Christians should be mindful of their example seen by the world – **1ˢᵗ Peter 2:11-12 TLB, MSG.**

Whether we want to be or not, we are examples to others, especially the young in years and young in faith. **So, what kind of example are we to others? We will study this further in our next lesson.**

Memory Verse: Titus 2:7: *"In all things showing yourself to be a pattern of good works; in doctrine showing integrity, reverence, incorruptibility."*

Monday, November 11th

ONE-YEAR BIBLE PLAN: EZEKIEL 21-22/ HEBREWS CH. 1&2

Matthew 8:14-15: *"…. Wife's mother laid, and sick of a fever. And he touched her hand, and the fever left her: and she arose, and ministered unto them."*

YOUR RELEVANCE

You may not know it, but walking in the miraculous is a function of your relevance in God's scheme of things. The more relevant you are to God, the more qualified you are for a miracle.

In 'Today's Scripture,' as soon as Jesus healed Peter's mother-in-law, she got up and ministered to them. Having gone around ministering to people all day, Jesus and His group were exhausted when they arrived at Peter's home. So, they needed someone to refresh them. But Peter's mother-in-law was not able to do so due to fever.

So, it became imperative for Jesus to heal her immediately, without prompting. If, like Peter's mother-in-law, you make yourself relevant and useful for God's purpose, you will always have a miracle. Be useful in the house of God, in evangelism, etc.

Are you one of the seatwarmers who care little about God's work? Are you one of those who do not contribute anything to advance God's work? If so, there is a need for you to change. Learn to make yourself relevant in the things of the kingdom, and the Lord will bless you without measure in Jesus' Name. Amen!

Prayer: *Lord, give me the grace to be useful in your kingdom.*

Tuesday, November 12th

ONE-YEAR BIBLE PLAN: EZEKIEL 23-24/ HEBREWS 3:1-19

Proverbs 4:23: *"Above all else, guard your heart, for everything you do flows from it."*

THE HEART

May Christ's love be the rhythm in your step and His grace the melody in your heart.

In Biblical terms, the heart refers to our emotions, thoughts, will, and innermost being. This proverb is a poignant reminder of the importance of guarding it. Just as the body's health can be determined by the state of the heart, the spiritual and emotional health of our lives can be gauged by the condition of our inner heart.

When our hearts are filled with God's love, grace, and truth, our actions and words will naturally reflect His light. But if we allow bitterness, envy, or negativity to take root, it can influence every aspect of our lives.

Guarding our heart is not about building walls but nurturing it with God's Word, surrounding ourselves with godly influences, and constantly checking our emotions and motives in the light of His truth.

What are you allowing into your heart and mind daily? How can you better shield your heart from negative influences and cultivate positive, Godly ones? Think about this!

Prayer: *Father, nourish my heart with Your Word, and let me be mindful of what I let in, always choosing love, truth, and all things that honor You. In the name of Jesus, Amen*

Wednesday, November 13th

ONE-YEAR BIBLE PLAN: EZEK. 25-26/ HEBREWS CH. 4&5

EXAMPLES WORTH FOLLOWING 5/5

III. WHAT KIND OF EXAMPLE ARE YOU?

A. IS IT INDICATIVE OF A FAITHFUL CHRISTIAN?

1. Are we showing the world what it means to be a Christian?
2. Are we showing babes in Christ what maturity means as a disciple?
3. Is your example helping or hindering discipleship in others?

B. IS IT CONDUCIVE TO CHURCH GROWTH?

1. Are we offering a noble pattern of faithful church attendance?
2. Are we setting a good example of developing our ability for Christ?
3. Are we worthy models of involvement in service to the Lord and His Church?
4. Is our example helping or hindering the progress of the church?

C. IS IT WORTHY OF EMULATION?

1. **Would you want a child or new Christian to follow your example?**
2. If every member provided the same example as you.
3. Would the church be strong?

4. Would the church grow?

5. Would the church have service on Sunday and Wednesday nights?

6. Would the church even exist?

7. Is your example helping or hindering the cause of Christ?

In conclusion, I hope these questions have prompted serious introspection on your part:

1. As to who is your example or role model as a Christian?

2. As to the example or role model you are setting for others!

3. Today, I encourage you to apply Paul's words to yourself. Be an example to the believers – **1ˢᵗ Timothy 4:12.**

4. Be an example in word, conduct, love, spirit, faith, purity – **1ˢᵗ Timothy 4:12b** *"...In spirit, in faith, in purity."*

5. **You cannot escape being an example to others.** Your only choice is what kind of example you will be. Will you be one of the many *"Examples Worth Following."*

Memory Verse: 1ˢᵗ Timothy 4:12: *"Let no one despise your youth, but be an example to the believers in word, in conduct, in love, in spirit, in faith, in purity."*

Thursday, November 14th

ONE-YEAR BIBLE PLAN: EZEKIEL 27-28/ HEBREWS 6:1-20

Philippians 2:9-10: *"Wherefore God also hath highly exalted him, and given him a name which is above every name: that at the name of Jesus, every knee should bow...."*

THE NAME

Once you decide to keep the commands of Jesus and allow the Word to dwell in you richly, the Name of Jesus will become far more powerful to you. It will become more than just words. It will become a force that will cause every circumstance and every demon that tries to stand in your way to bow at your command.

I tell you, the Name of Jesus works. It has far greater power than any of us have yet realized. My faith is so set on the authority of the Name of Jesus that there are times I say, "In the Name," and the power of God comes on the scene. I've discovered that the Name of Jesus—just the Name alone—is effective when spoken by a Word-abiding believer.

Revelation 19:13 says *the Name of Jesus is the Word of God!* So, when an evil spirit is trying to bring sickness, poverty, depression, or any other garbage into my household, I don't have to quote every scripture to stop him. I can point my finger at him and say, "Jesus!" That's like throwing the whole Word of God in his face at once.

Discover for yourself what the exalted Name can do. Begin to speak it with confidence and authority. There is power in the Name of Jesus.

Prayer: *"In the Name of Jesus, all my problems must bow!*

Friday, November 15th

ONE-YEAR BIBLE PLAN: EZEKIEL 29-30/ HEBREWS 7:1-28

Philippians 4:13 AMPC: *"I have strength for all things in Christ Who empowers me [I am ready for anything and equal to anything through Him Who infuses inner strength into me; I am self-sufficient in Christ's sufficiency]."*

READY

Have you ever been worried that you weren't ready for something you had to do? **Philippians 4:13** promises that Christ will empower you for every situation you face. He'll prepare you for anything and give you what you need for every challenge by infusing you with inner strength.

God will never put you in a position to do something without giving you the grace and the ability to do it, so don't stress. You can trust Him to equip you with exactly what you need daily.

Relax and enjoy your life because God will strengthen you completely and perfectly and make you what you should be. He will equip you with everything good that you may carry out His will; [while He] works in you and accomplishes that which is pleasing in His sight, through Jesus Christ **Hebrews 13:21 AMPC.**

Prayer:

Father, please help me trust You a little more today than yesterday—I know You love and want to help me. Thank You for giving me exactly what I need to deal with every situation I face today. In Jesus' Name, Amen.

Saturday, November 16th

ONE-YEAR BIBLE PLAN: EZEKIEL 31-32/ HEBREWS 8:1-13

WISDOM OF THE ORACLE

WHAT YOU WANT

What goal excites you? What do you dream of becoming when you are alone and away from everyone else? When people hear your name spoken, what do they automatically think of? What legacy do you want to pass on to others?

Many need to learn what they want. They do not realize that their dream is either born within them or borrowed from someone else. How disappointing that most people never pursue their inner passion. But that person does not have to be you. Your dream is closer than you can imagine. Your dream is completely obtainable. Recognize it. Embrace it. Pursue it. This is your season to do something significant with your life.

- o If you don't know what you want, who do you Ask? If you don't know where you belong, you will adapt to where you are.
- o Solomon was the richest man who ever lived. He knew what he wanted. He was passionate about his Dream.
- o Passionate people become powerful people. Passionate people create excitement and enthusiasm.
- o Passionate people generate waves of favor that naturally attract access and promotion. Be passionate about what you want.

Third Sunday in November 17th

ONE-YEAR BIBLE PLAN: EZEKIEL 33-34/ HEBREWS 9:1-28

WHAT SHALL I WEAR? 1/6

"What shall I wear?" It is a question we all ask nearly every day. As we dress for work, or to relax, or other outings activities, etc. It usually considers fashion, form, style, substance, the occasion, and weather. When Christians ask this question, other issues should come into consideration. **Is it modest? Is this outfit proper for emulation as a Christian for others? Is it proper for the one professing godliness? - 1st Timothy 2:9-10 AMPC; MSG; NIV.**

The challenge is what constitutes modesty constantly changes. It was immodest for a woman to expose her ankle at one time. Today, even the most modest of dress would have been considered scandalous.

So, the question remains, "What Shall I Wear?

Should a Christian woman wear shorts, mini-skirts, low-cut blouses, tight skirts, or pants? Should we be concerned about modest apparel? How might this affect certain activities, such as mixed swimming and other athletic sports?

There is no easy answer or simple guideline such as "no higher than an inch above the knee." Rather, we are to prayerfully consider what the Bible says, which provides basic principles to help us discern between good and evil. *In this new series, God will give us understanding in the Name of Jesus Christ. Amen!*

Memory Verse: 1st Timothy 2:9-10

Monday, November 18th

ONE-YEAR BIBLE PLAN: EZEKIEL 35-36/ HEBREWS 10:1-39

Exodus 15:2: *"The LORD is my strength and song, and he is my salvation: he is my God ...."*

NO FEAR

Psalm 3:6 says, *"I will not be afraid of ten thousand people that have set themselves against me roundabout."*

2nd Timothy 1:7: *"For God hath not given us the spirit of fear, but of power, and love, and a sound mind:"*

You are created to live dangerously. God created you to live an adventurous life, not to be prey. You are fearfully and wonderfully made. God made you in His image - bold in everything you do; God made you a warrior like He is. The scripture calls Him warrior, mighty man of war, the Lord of host. You are an eagle, not a chicken, a predator, not a prey. But you are not a predator to prey on the weak but against the power of darkness.

When our Lord Jesus was here on earth, tough as He is, He never went about intimidating and bossing people around. Jesus Christ loves; He is caring and lives from a servant's heart. No matter your attainment in life, secularly or in ministry, true confidence is inherent in the confidence from the spiritual genes inherited from your heavenly father.

Living boldly is nothing more than being in the realization of who you are in Christ Jesus and knowing and doing what God demands from you at all times. Pray now!

Prayer: *"Lord Jesus, cast out the spirit fear out of my life. Please give me the courage to live boldly every day!*

Tuesday, November 19th

ONE-YEAR BIBLE PLAN: EZEKIEL 37-38/ HEBREWS 10:1-39

1st Corinthians 15:34: *"Awake to righteousness, and sin not...."*

WAKE UP TO RIGHTEOUSNESS

When your alarm clock goes off in the morning, don't just wake up to another day. Do what the Word says to do and "awake to righteousness"! Reawaken yourself to the glorious truth that you've been made the righteousness of God in Christ Jesus and given right standing with God.

Why? Because tomorrow—and every day of your life on this earth—Satan is going to try to convince you that you don't have any right to the things of God. He's going to try to bring you into bondage again to sin to control your life. But he can't do it if you'll reawaken yourself daily to who you are in Jesus.

Here's a prayerful confession to help that revelation come alive in you:

PRAY NOW

"Father, I confess anew Jesus Christ as my Lord and Savior today. Lord, You are the head of my life. I completely yield myself to You. My will is now Your will. My plans are now Your plans. "I determine today to walk conscious of my right standing with You, Lord, and with every step to draw closer and closer to You. Thank You for the gift of righteousness. Because of that gift, I can do everything through Christ, strengthening me. In Jesus' Name. Amen!"

Wednesday, November 20th

ONE-YEAR BIBLE PLAN: EZEKIEL 39-40/ HEBREWS 11:1-40

WHAT SHALL I WEAR? 2/6

I. IT IS SHAMEFUL TO EXPOSE ONE'S NAKEDNESS:

A. LET'S CONSIDER THE EXAMPLE OF ADAM AND EVE:

After they sinned, they made "coverings" for themselves – **Genesis 3:7-10.**

The Hebrew word for dress or cloth is "Chagorah," meaning a garment that covers the midsection.

Note that despite such coverings of Adam and Eve, they still felt naked! Then the Lord made "tunics" for them in - **Genesis 3:21 AMPC.**

The Hebrew word for tunics or long coats is "ketones," a garment reaching the knee. God was not pleased with the brevity of the coverings they had made for themselves.

Think about what you wear.

Will it be pleasing to God?

Will God approve of what you wear?

Memory Verse: Genesis 3:21: *"Also for Adam and his wife the Lord God made tunics of skin, and clothed them."*

Thursday, November 21ˢᵗ

ONE-YEAR BIBLE PLAN: EZEK. 41-42 / HEBREWS 12:1-29

Matthew 21:22: *"If you believe, you will receive whatever you ask for in prayer."*

ASK IN PRAYER

Another day is before you, and it's not just any day—it's designed by God, filled with His promises and possibilities. As you sip your morning coffee or tea, focus on a promise that can redefine how you approach life.

When you read today's verse, it's easy to think it's too good to be true. But God doesn't make promises lightly. This powerful statement about prayer and faith isn't just poetic; it's practical. It tells us that belief isn't just a mental exercise but a potent force that activates God's promises in our lives.

This isn't about getting whatever we want, like some spiritual vending machine. It's about aligning our will with God's will, believing He can and will act according to His loving and perfect plan for us. When faith becomes the cornerstone of your prayer life, doors of healing, peace, and unexpected blessings swing wide open.

How strong is your faith when you pray to God?

Are you fully trusting in His promises and timing, or are there areas of doubt that you need to surrender to Him?

How can you align your will more closely with God's will in your prayer life today? Meditate on these questions.

Prayer:

"Lord, help my unbelief in Jesus' Name. Amen!

Friday, November 22nd

ONE-YEAR BIBLE PLAN: EZEKIEL 43-44 / HEBREWS 12:1-29

John 6:51: *"I am the living bread that came down from heaven ...."*

BREAD OF LIFE

In **John 6:48,** we read that Jesus said, *"I am the bread of life."*

Jesus had just fed 5,000 people with five loaves and two fishes. They were all excited and thrilled over the great miracle, [but] Jesus was talking about something more important than social needs.

Bread in the Scriptures is a symbol of spiritual life.

Man has an inborn hunger for God. He cannot be satisfied with anything less than God. God alone can supply the bread which satisfies your soul's inner longing and heart's hunger. . ... The Bible says that He is the Bread of Life.

Prayer:

Lord Jesus, thank You for deepening the yearnings in my heart. Your presence fulfills the needs of my soul, and I rejoice.

Saturday, November 23rd

ONE-YEAR BIBLE PLAN: EZEKIEL 45-46/ HEBREWS 13:1-25

WISDOM OF THE ORACLE

LEADING AND LEARNING

- Ever learning is ever leading.
- You can't be learning and not be leading.
- Only those who learn well will lead well.
- Any dummy can lead if he takes the time to learn what leaders do.
- It never becomes your turn to lead, except you make it your turn to learn – learning puts you on the line of leadership.

Fourth Sunday in November

ONE-YEAR BIBLE PLAN: EZEKIEL 47-48/ JAMES 1:1-27

WHAT SHALL I WEAR? 3/6

I. IT IS SHAMEFUL TO EXPOSE ONE'S NAKEDNESS:

B. IT IS ALSO SHAMEFUL TO EXPOSE OR DRAW ATTENTION TO PRIVATE PARTS OF THE BODY: Exposure of such parts was often a form of judgment intended to shame the wicked - **Isaiah 3:16-17 AMPC; MSG; TLB; Isaiah 47:1-3 AMPC; NIV; MSG.**

Paul alludes that some parts are "unpresentable" and should be covered – **1st Corinthians 12:23-24 AMPC; TLB.**

At some point, there needs to be a line where it is a shame to cross; there are parts of the body that should remain private.

Perhaps we can begin to determine what these may be as we consider another principle in our next lesson:

> **Memory Verse: 1st Corinthians 6:19-20:** *"Do you not know that your bodies are temples of the Holy Spirit, who is in you, whom you have received from God? You are not your own; 20, you were bought at a price. Therefore, honor God with your bodies."*

Monday, November 25th

ONE-YEAR BIBLE PLAN: DANIEL 1-2 / JAMES 2:1-26

Psalm 100:4-5: *"Enter into His gate with thanksgiving, and into His court with praise: be thankful unto Him, and bless His name. For our God is good......"*

FORGET NOT HIS BENEFIT

Since we shouted Happy New Year ten months ago, many people have died. We aren't better than them! It is of the mercy of the Lord that we are not consumed!

David said, *"Bless the Lord O my soul.... and forget not all His benefits.* Human memory can be very short, particularly regarding good things. We tend to remember bad things more. If you are grateful for whatever benefit you received in the past, your attitude of gratitude will make room for more benefits for you. Have a grateful heart towards God and bless Him for life.

PRAYER OF THANKSGIVING!

Lord, I thank You for sustenance, preservation, and protection! Thank You for Life! I Thank You for Your mercies that endure forever! I am not in any way better or superior to those who are dead; by Your mercy, O Lord, I am not consumed. I bless You, Lord, for all Your benevolence towards me! I thank you for the healing, deliverances, and victories of the past! I will Count my blessings one by one! Thank You for Your faithfulness! I thank You, Lord, from the bottom of my heart! I give You all the glory and adoration! I give You all honor! Thank You for loving me in Jesus' Name. Amen

Tuesday, November 26th

ONE-YEAR BIBLE PLAN: DANIEL 3-4 / JAMES CH. 3&4

Luke 22:42: *"Saying, Father, if thou be willing, remove this cup from me: nevertheless, not my will, but thine, be done."*

HIS WILL

Jesus knew it was the Father's will for Him to be made an offering for the world's sins. However, because of His unique relationship with God, Jesus asked God to accomplish His will some other way while affirming His commitment to do His Father's will and not His own. He was not at a loss as to God's will, thus trusting that whatever the Father deemed best for Him would happen. When He began praying, He knew what the Father's will was, and He knew at the close of His prayer that God's will could not be accomplished any other way.

For us to pray, *'Lord, if it be thy will'* in response to a promise God has given us is nothing but unbelief and is not even remotely related to what Jesus did in the Garden of Gethsemane. One of the principles of answered prayer is that we must believe that we receive when we pray **Mark 11:24.** There is no way we can fulfill that condition if we don't know God's will in that situation.

Praying, *'if it is thy will,'* takes us out of the active position of believing and puts us in the passive position of waiting and letting circumstances rule our lives. If we seek direction in an area where God's will is not expressed in His Word, we should pray **James 1:5** and ask for wisdom. Then, we can believe that we receive when we pray.

Prayer: *"I believe I shall receive as I pray in Jesus' Name!*

Wednesday, November 27th

ONE-YEAR BIBLE PLAN: DANIEL 5-6 /JAMES 5:1-20

WHAT SHALL I WEAR? 4/6

II. WE MUST NOT CREATE OPPORTUNITIES FOR LUST.

A. THIS IS CONDEMNED IN THE SCRIPTURES: Romans 13:13-14 NIV; MSG.

Can the way we dress excite fleshly lusts?

- a) **Many think that women are more attractive partly dressed - than nude.** They prefer to see women partially disrobed to the sight of complete nakedness.

- b) **Mini clothes are symbolic of those girls who want to seduce a man.**

- c) **During the hijacking of the Santa Maria in 1961, the women on board the cruise ship were concerned the rebels might have desire on them,** so they left off wearing "enticing clothing"; i.e., they stopped wearing shorts and minis and quit swimming in the ship's pool.

If the "women of the world" know what can stimulate the lust of the flesh, why not the "daughters of God"?

B. JESUS WARNED ABOUT "COMMITTING ADULTERY IN THE HEART": Matthew 5:27-30.

There is a two-fold responsibility here:

  I.   **The man is responsible for guarding** his mind from impurity: Philippians 4:8.

II. **Women are to help prevent the lewd stare.** Though lust is inexcusable on the man's part, if the woman, by her apparel or conduct, has encouraged it, she shares in the guilt! - e.g., **Proverbs 7:6-27.**

If our clothing encourages the arousal of fleshly lusts in others, then we have crossed the line.

And, of course, this requires honesty and objectivity on our part; we must be willing to be true to ourselves and God.

So, to help us toward that end, we shall consider another basic principle from God's Word in our next lesson.

Memory Verse: Matthew 5:28: *"But I say to you that whoever looks at a woman to lust for her has already committed adultery with her in his heart."*

Thursday, November 28th

ONE-YEAR BIBLE PLAN: DANIEL 7-8 / 1ST PETER 1:1-25

Lamentations 3:22-23: *"Because of the Lord's great love, we are not consumed, for his compassions never fail. They are new every morning; great is your faithfulness."*

FAITHFUL GOD

As the sunrise brightens the world, let God's faithful promises light up your heart today. Daily, we're wrapped in His care, reminded that His kindness and love are as sure as the morning. No matter what challenges or surprises this day holds, we can be anchored in this remarkable truth - God's mercies are new every morning. His compassion will always stay, so do not grow weary, and be sure to maintain enthusiasm. At each sunrise, His grace is miraculously refreshed and available to us.

Wherever today leads you - mountaintops of celebration or valleys of weariness - take comfort knowing you do not walk alone. God is with you, ready to lift you, carry you through, and speak peace and love. For His faithful love transcends every season and circumstance.

Ask yourself how you can awaken your heart to receive God's new mercies daily. Ask yourself whether you are boldly embracing His mercy.

Prayer:

Father, as sunrise illuminates this new day, I rejoice that Your mercies are fresh and new once more. Where I feel weary, breathe renewal into my soul. Let Your compassion eclipse all fear when doubts arise in Jesus' Name. Amen!

Friday, November 29th

ONE-EAR BIBLE PLAN: DANIEL 9-10 / 1ST PETER 2:1-25

Ephesians 2:11-13: *"...But now in Christ Jesus ye who sometimes was far off are made nigh by the Blood of Christ."*

DEFEAT THE DEVIL

Have you ever thought about what being in Christ Jesus means? Have you ever gotten a clear revelation of that? Once you do, it will revolutionize your life.

It's in Him that we're raised from our sins. It's in Him that we're made to sit in heavenly places so that God can show us the exceeding riches of His grace. It's in Him that we're made the righteousness of God!

If you want that revelation to explode, start searching out scriptures that refer to being in Christ. **Watch for the words in Him, with Him, through Him, or in whom.** Mark and meditate on them until their truth gets down into your spirit.

They'll give you some powerful ammunition against the attacks of Satan. When he tries to tell you, for instance, that you're just a sinner and God doesn't want to be bothered with your problems, you'll know he is lying. You'll be able to answer him boldly and say, *"Thank God, I was a sinner, but now I'm the righteousness of God in Christ Jesus. I've been raised to sit with Him in heavenly places. Now I'm in Him, and you can't touch me!"* Be prepared the next time Satan comes at you with condemnation. Be ready to fight back with the scriptures about who you are in Jesus. You're sure to win once you truly know you're in Him!

Saturday, November 30th

ONE-YEAR BIBLE PLAN: DANIEL 11-12 / 1ST PETER 3:1-22

WISDOM OF THE ORACLE

ATTITUDE IS POWERFUL

- A man's attitude defines his ratings.
- It determines his placement.
- Your attitude attracts people to you or repels them from you.
- Your attitude is your real representation.
- You cannot subdue it; it will naturally reveal who you are.
- Change your attitude to enhance your altitude.

First Sunday in December

ONE-YEAR BIBLE PLAN: HOSEA 1-2 /1ˢᵀ PETER 4:1-19

WHAT SHALL I WEAR? 5/6

III. CLOTHING MUST BE CONSISTENT WITH GODLINESS.

A. CONSIDER CAREFULLY 1ˢᵗ TIMOTHY 2:9-10 TLB; NIV; NKJV.

The Greek word for **"modest"** is **[kosmio]**, which means "Orderly, well arranged, decent, modest" **[akin to kosmos]**. In its primary sense, it means "harmonious arrangement adornment"; the **kosmikos** of the world, which is related to kosmos in its secondary sense as the world.

"The well-ordering is not of dress and demeanor only, but of the inner life, uttering in deeds and expressing itself in the outward conversation." In this context, this word applies not so much to the brevity of clothing but to the ostentation of clothing. Modesty is used regarding the demeanor of women in the church. This word applies more to the issue of the brevity of clothing:

In Greek, decency, decorum, or "propriety" is **[aidos]**. Translated "shamefacedness" in the **KJV**. " A sense of shame. So, we can say that those who display their bodies to excite lust in others have the quality of "shamefacedness"?

The Greek word for **"moderation"** is **[sophrosune]**. It translated as "sobriety" in the **KJV**. It "denotes soundness of mind. It is that habitual inner self-government, with its constant rein on all the passions and desires, which would hinder temptation from arising."

A sound mind considers the effect one's clothes have on others. The Bible says, *"not with braided hair, gold, pearls or costly clothing."* Rather than actual adornment, the excess is condemned here - **Isaiah 3:16-26 NIV; MSG; Ezekiel 16:9-14 NIV.**

This is an example of the comparative use of "not" found frequently in the Bible:

I.   "Not" is sometimes used absolutely - **Exodus 20:14** *"Thou shalt not commit adultery."*

II. "Not" is sometimes used conditionally **[not...if]** - **Galatians 5:21.**

III. "Not" is sometimes used comparatively **[not...but]** - **John 6:27.**

Outward adornment is correct, but it is of lower priority and lesser importance than the adorning of the inner person by good works. But that *"proper for women professing godliness"* is fitting, seemly, suitable, becoming – **Ephesians 5:3-7; Titus 2:1 AMPC.**

For women claiming to be reverent, pious - **Titus 2:3-5**

Would a woman who professes to be godly knowingly adorn herself in a way that excites lust in another person?

Memory Verse: 1ˢᵗ Corinthians 10:31: *"So whether you eat or drink or whatever you do, do it all for the glory of God."*

Monday, December 2nd

ONE-YEAR BIBLE PLAN: HOSEA 3-4 / 1ST PETER 5:1-14

Psalm 67:5: *"Let the peoples praise You, O God; let all the peoples praise You."*

PRAISE GOD!

If God had not been on our side when the enemy rose against us, they would have swallowed us. Praise God for being your defender, your Protector, the One fighting your battles. Worship Him for being your Provider! Praise Him for loving you. Express your appreciation of His love by praising Him as you have never done! Praise and worship Him; magnify His Holy Name! Show Him that you love Him with praise.

PRAISE THE LORD!

Father, King of Glory; Ancient of Days, Unchangeable Lord, from everlasting to everlasting, You are God! I magnify Your Holy Name. You are the Almighty! There is no one like You! Therefore, I adore You! In Jesus' Name. Amen!

BIRTHDAY AND ANNIVERSARY PRAYERS

Father, I commit all your children born this month and those celebrating an anniversary to your hands. As they begin a New Year, answer their prayers speedily. Do something new for them. Give them new joy, new blessings, and breakthrough testimonies. Perfect all that concerns them in Jesus' Name. Amen!

Tuesday, December 3rd

ONE-YEAR BIBLE PLAN: HOSEA 5-6 / 2ND PETER 1:1-21

2nd Timothy 3:14: *"But continue thou in the things which thou hast learned and hast been assured of, knowing of whom thou hast learned them."*

THE LIGHT YOU HAVE

You can live in victory if you're born again and have God's Word in your heart. You may not have all the answers. There may be a great many spiritual things you don't understand. But it's not those things that are most likely to destroy you.

Just think about walking down a dark, unfamiliar path in the middle of a jungle at night. The guide up ahead has a flashlight to keep you on the right path. But then, you decide to wander off into the darkness by yourself. What do you think will happen to you? That's the same thing that can happen in your walk with the Lord. He knows what's ahead and shines just enough light for you to take one step at a time.

You must continue walking in that light to get where you're going. You may not know why He's leading you a certain way. But God will make up for your ignorance by the Holy Spirit. He'll see you have victory if you continue with what you know. It's good to keep studying. It's good to keep learning. But remember, it's not the great revelation you haven't yet had that will cause you the most trouble. It's failing to walk in the ones God has already given you. So be faithful in those things. *Continue in them day after day after day. You'll make it through just fine, in Jesus' Name. Amen!*

Wednesday, December 4th

ONE-YEAR BIBLE PLAN: HOSEA 7-8 / 2ND PETER 2:1-22

WHAT SHALL I WEAR? 6/6

III. CLOTHING MUST BE CONSISTENT WITH GODLINESS

B. LET'S ALSO CONSIDER: 1st Peter 3:1-6.

Note first the potential value of chaste conduct – **1st Peter 3:1-2 TLB.**

Good behavior can influence one for good; likewise, improper behavior [like immodest clothing] can have an adverse effect!

In **verses 3-4 NIV,** we have another example of the comparative use of **"not":** *"Whose adorning let it not be that outward adorning of plaiting the hair, and of wearing of gold, or of putting on of apparel; But let it be the hidden man of the heart, in that which is not corruptible, even the ornament of a meek and quiet spirit, which is in the sight of God of great price."*

The emphasis should not be one's adornment [arranging the hair, wearing gold, putting on apparel]. Rather, it should be adorning one's inner person.

The adornment that greatly pleases God. The incorruptible beauty of a gentle and quiet spirit. As worn by women like Sarah, who trusted God and submitted to her husband – **1st Peter 3:4-6 TLB; MSG.**

When a person disregards the effect their apparel may have on another, can it be said they are adorned with a gentle and quiet spirit?

In conclusion, it is not my goal to establish specific rules for modest dressing. To do so would be to do what the Bible itself does not do. Rather, this study offers general principles that can help us who desire to please God rather than self or man.

When faced with the question "What shall I wear?"

1. Prayerfully consider whether your adornment reflects your profession of godliness and the principles found in God's word.

2. Seek counsel from those mature in the faith whose senses have been exercised to discern good and evil. **Hebrews 5:14**

If we do this, we are more likely to fulfill that goal set for us by the Apostle Paul that we are. *"...blameless and harmless, children of God without fault amid a crooked and perverse generation, among whom you shine as lights in the world."* **Philippians 2:15.**

Memory Verse: Philippians 2:15: *"That you may become blameless and harmless, children of God without fault in a crooked and perverse generation, among whom you shine as lights in the world."*

Thursday, December 5th

ONE-YEAR BIBLE PLAN: HOSEA 9-10 / 2ND PETER 3:1-18

Isaiah 40:31: *"But they that wait upon the Lord shall renew their strength..."*

HE KNOWS YOUR NEED

It is an exhilarating experience to live a new life, with Christ inside you enabling you to live it.

As a man rode along in his Ford, something suddenly went wrong. He got out and looked at the engine but found nothing wrong. As he stood there, another car appeared, and he waved it down to ask for help. A tall, friendly man stepped out of a brand-new Lincoln and asked, "Well, what's the trouble?" "I cannot get this car to move," was the reply. The stranger made a few adjustments under the hood and said, "Now start the car." When the motor started, its grateful owner introduced himself and asked, "What is your name, sir?" "My name," answered the stranger, "is Henry Ford."

The one who made the Ford knew how to make it run. God made us; He alone knows how to run our lives. We could make a complete wreck of our lives without Christ. When He is in control, all goes well. Without Him, we can do nothing.

Prayer:

I must remember to give You complete control so often, and I fail. Teach me to rely completely on You for my strength and needs.

Friday, December 6th

ONE-YEAR BIBLE PLAN: HOSEA 11 / 1ST JOHN CH. 1&2

Mark 11:2: *"And saith unto them, Go your way into the village against you: and as soon as ye be entered into it, ye shall find a colt tied, whereon never man sat; lose him, and bring him."*

TRUST NOT THE GIFT

The gifts of the Spirit do not substitute for our faith in the Lord. We are not to depend so completely on someone with a spiritual gift that we neglect our spiritual growth and maturity. We can receive anything we need from God without a gift of the Spirit operating through another individual if we believe. Dependence on the Lord directly is superior to dependence indirectly through someone operating spiritual gifts.

What if no gifts of the Spirit and the Lord were established that we could only receive from Him through our faith? It is wrong for an individual not to mature in his faith in the Lord and become dependent on the gifts. It is not right for someone to receive a miracle through someone with the gift of miracles and then struggle until the next time that gifted minister comes through town.

God wants us to receive His power through these gifts, but we must mature to walk in God's best. We can mature beyond a total dependency on the gifts to where we can receive from God directly. But we will only reach such a level of maturity by lean on the Lord. Let Him teach you through His Word today.

Prayer: *I will not solely depend on the gift but the giver of the gift.*

Saturday, December 7th

ONE-YEAR BIBLE PLAN: HOSEA 12 / 1ST JOHN CH. 3&4

WISDOM OF THE ORACLE

TESTIMONY IMPACT

- Testimonies are the foremost pieces of evidence of impact.
- If you are truly touching lives, they will testify.
- Good word can never be equal to great touch.
- Don't be excited about people's comments about your messages but about the impact your message is making on them.
- Your good message may be forgotten, but your impact will be preserved in their minds.
- Please don't wait for people to greet you; you don't need it!

Second Sunday in December

ONE-YEAR BIBLE PLAN: HOSEA 13 / 1ST JOHN CH. 3&4

NEW CHRISTIANS DISAPPOINTMENTS 1/3

There is great joy in seeing New Christians grow in the faith – **2nd John 4; 3rd John 3-4 NIV.**

Unfortunately, not all New Believers grow as they should - **Luke 8:11-14 TLB.**

Problems and disappointments often overwhelm them, and some even fall away. This should concern older Christians, for we are responsible to those young in the faith – **Galatians 6:1-2; Romans 15:1-2 AMPC.**

This lesson is designed to help us understand and deal with some disappointments that New Christians face.

For example, a problem that is troubling to some is:

I. SAME WEAKNESSES AS BEFORE

A. MANY BECOME CHRISTIANS WITH JOYFUL ANTICIPATION – Acts 8:39.

Excited about forgiveness of sins:

Excited about the chance to start over:

Excited about the help God is going to give them to change:

B. BUT WHEN THEY SOON DISCOVER: The temptations are just as strong as before, sometimes even stronger! They are disappointed with themselves. And become easily discouraged and overcome – **Luke 8:13 AMPC; MSG; TLB.**

HOW CAN WE HELP?

#1. Teaching them that "transformation" is an ongoing process - **Romans 12:1-2 AMPC TLB; MSG; Colossians 3:5-11 AMPC.**

#2. Reminding them of God's willingness to forgive and provide strength – **1ˢᵗ John 1:9 MSG; AMPC; 1ˢᵗ John 2:1 AMPC; 1ˢᵗ John 3:8-9 AKJV; Philippians 2:12-13 TLB; AMPC.**

A stumbling block to many new Christians is what we shall study in our next lesson:

Memory Verse: Philippians 2:12-13: *"Therefore, my beloved, as you have always obeyed, not as in my presence only, but now much more in my absence, work out your salvation with fear and trembling; for it is God who works in you both to will and to do for His good pleasure."*

Monday, December 9th

ONE-YEAR BIBLE PLAN: HOSEA 14 / 1ST JOHN 5:1-21

Isaiah 60:1-3: *".... and gross darkness ... but the LORD shall arise upon thee, and his glory shall be seen upon thee......."*

ARISE AND SHINE

Negative consciousness is one of the most encountered behavioral trends in people I counsel. The average counselee has a pre-negated mindset, perhaps due to the world's negative polarity. Humans are very predisposed to negativity.

On several occasions, I have seen and listened to people who never see anything positive in life. The truth is that unless such people change their perceptions, they will never get anything out of life. In life, what you see is what you get. Without vision, you perish. As a believer, you are supposed to focus on God's ability, which is your only responsibility. Do not stare at your situation. Rather, look over them and focus on God. **Job 22:29** says, *"When men are cast down, then thou shalt say, there is lifting ...."*

Beloved, know this day that your fate depends not on the economic index of this world or the ability or capability of any human being. Rather, as a person born of the Spirit of God, your life's progress and promotion are in God's hands, the author and the finisher of your faith and fate. The Almighty is the sole determining factor of your destiny and destination. *So, you must rise and shine when others experience darkness, and so shall it be in Jesus' Mighty name. Amen.*

Prayer: *"I shall arise and shine in Jesus' Name. Amen!*

Tuesday, December 10th

ONE-YEAR BIBLE PLAN: JOEL 1-3 / 2ND JOHN 1:1-13.

Romans 12:12: *"Be joyful in hope, patient in affliction, faithful in prayer."*

HOPE IN GOD

Welcome, today, with a heart ready to soak in God's hope, trusting His loving plans for you to unfold.

Romans 12:12 is a compass for your soul, guiding you through varied life landscapes. It calls us to embrace the joy that doesn't just bubble up on easy days but also on the tough ones because our hope is anchored in something eternal.

Patience in affliction is our quiet strength, a serene steadiness that weathers life's storms, not because we are undaunted but because we trust God's sovereignty. And through it all, our constant dialogue with the Lord—prayer—ties our daily walk tightly to His purpose and presence.

Today, let these words shape how you meet every moment. Let joy, patience, and faithfulness be the markers of your journey, knowing that each step is shared with the One who calls you His own.

Prayer: *I pray for protection and guidance on this day. Protect my family and me from anything that may bring harm to us. Guide me, Lord, help me remember that your plans are greater than mine. Draw me closer to you, Lord, so that I may walk in your will this week. In Jesus' Name. Amen.*

Wednesday, December 11th

ONE-YEAR BIBLE PLAN: AMOS 1-2 / 3ʳᴰ JOHN 1:1-14

NEW CHRISTIANS DISAPPOINTMENTS 2/3

II. IMPERFECT CHRISTIANS

A. THEY WITNESS INCONSISTENCY IN THE LIVES OF OTHERS: They see those who do not practice what they preach. It hurts when New Christians see the opposite of their expectation in those they had looked up to for a positive change. They are disappointed by their brethren. But this problem is common - **Galatians 2:11-14 AMPC; TLB.**

1. First, set better examples! – **1ˢᵗ Timothy 4:12 AMPC.**

2. Confess wrong when it occurs. This helps the New Christian realize that older Christians are also going through the process of "transformation" - **Philippians 3:12-14 AMPC.**

Then there is the problem of:

III. TRIALS AND TEMPTATIONS.

A. SUCH AS PLEASURES AND RESPONSIBILITIES OF THE WORLD: Often drawing the new Christian away, e.g., job, family, hobbies, and choking them to the point of unfruitfulness. They become disappointed by the world - **Luke 8:14 AMPC.**

B. DISCOURAGEMENT BY UNCOVERTED FRIENDS: Who wants them to return to the things of the world? As Paul warned in **1ˢᵗ Corinthians 15:33 AMPC; TLB.**

C. WHAT CAN WE DO?

#1. Demonstrate what it means to *"seek first the kingdom of God"* - **Matthew 6:33.**

#2. Make it clear by our example who we love the most, i.e., not our jobs, hobbies, etc. – **1st John 2:15-17 AMPC.**

#3. Develop close friendships with New Christians in the Lord: Friendships centered around Christ and His work, not just social interests.

Due to much misinformation about the Christian life, another problem some New Christians have is:

IV. FALSE CONCEPT OF PROSPERITY [Disappointed by lack of success].

A. THINKING THAT NOW ALL THEIR PROBLEMS WILL GO AWAY: An idea propagated by the **"gospel of health and wealth"** teachers and preachers. But such is not always the case, even as it was in the days of the first-century church– **1st Peter 1:6-9 AMPC; TLB; James 1:2-4; TLB; Ecclesiastes 7:13-14 TLB.**

B. WE NEED TO PREPARE NEW CHRISTIANS FOR POSSIBLE ADVERSITY. Even as Paul did - **Acts 14:21-22 AMPC; 2nd Timothy 3:12 NIV.**

This need is especially important because Satan often strikes hardest when one is new in the faith.

Memory Verse: 2nd Timothy 3:12: *"Yes, and all who desire to live godly in Christ Jesus will suffer persecution."*

Thursday, December 12th

ONE-YEAR BIBLE PLAN: AMOS 3-4 / JUDE 1:1-25

Philippians 3:10 AMPC: *"[For my determined purpose is] that I may know Him [that I may progressively become more deeply and intimately acquainted with Him, perceiving and recognizing and understanding the wonders of His Person more strongly and more clearly], and that I may in that same way come to know the power outflowing from His resurrection."*

YOUR PLACE

The more you fellowship with God in His Word, the more you'll know the "power of His resurrection." You'll develop joy. You'll develop faith. You'll start developing God's characteristics...just by fellowshipping with Him. You'll begin to understand who you are in Jesus.

One day, I was reading the story of the woman with the issue of blood who touched the hem of Jesus' garment and was healed. I'd read the story many times and pictured myself as almost everyone in the story, just experiencing how it would feel to be someone in the crowd or even the one who was healed.

Suddenly, God spoke to my spirit and said, Read that again, and this time, picture yourself as the one wearing the garment. I was stunned. "Lord," I said, "how can I do that? I can't take Your place!" He told me that's just what's wrong with the Body of Christ.

That's the reason the world doesn't know anything about Jesus. You identify with everyone except Me. But I sent you to be My witnesses, imitate Me, and stand in My place...not everyone else's!

So, I read that story again. This time, I pictured myself as the one with the Anointing of the Holy Ghost. Instead of crawling up to touch the hem of His garment, I was the one wearing the garment, freely giving what God had given me. After all, the Bible does say, *"Clothe yourself with the Lord Jesus Christ."*

Do you know who scares the devil most of all? Believers who've found out they can do that. Believers who, instead of begging for a little touch from Jesus, are letting His very life flow out to others. Come on, subsequently, give the devil a scare. Fellowship with your Father around the Word and discover who you are today.

Prayer:

I clothe my life in Christ Jesus!

Friday, December 13th

ONE-YEAR BIBLE PLAN: AMOS 5-6 / REVELATION 2:1-27

Exodus 4:11-12 AMPC: *"And the Lord said to him, Who has made man's mouth? Or who makes the dumb, or the deaf, or the seeing, or the blind? Is it not I, the Lord? Now, go, and I will be with your mouth and teach you what you shall say."*

IN GOD'S STRENGTH

The Bible is full of the stories of people God called to serve Him who didn't know what they were doing and were certainly less-than-qualified for a mission from God.

God's tool chest is full of weak, imperfect individuals who can't seem to get things right, those the world sees as basically worthless **1st Corinthians 1:28.**

But He knows something the world doesn't: that these people will look to Him for strength. And because they depend on Him, He can show Himself strong in their lives *"so that no mortal man should have pretense for glorying and boast in the presence of God."* **1st Corinthians 1:29 AMPC.**

You can qualify yourself for God's tool chest today by authentically sharing with others about your struggles and how He's worked in and through your life.

Prayer:

Father, help me to keep a humble attitude and look to You for my strength. Thank You for working through me in amazing ways despite my weaknesses and mistakes. In Jesus' Name. Amen.

Saturday, December 14th

ONE-YEAR BIBLE PLAN: Amos 7-9 / Revelation 3:1-22

WISDOM OF THE ORACLE

REWARDABLE SERVICE

- o Serving God heartily and actively are both required for rewardable services, but hearty service is more fundamental.
- o God sees the state of the heart, but men notice the act.
- o Our heart reaches Him before our acts.
- o Men may commend your acts, which are visible to all, but only God can commend your hearts because only Him can access them. **1st Samuel 16:7; 2nd Chronicles 16:9; Jeremiah 17:9-10.**

Third Sunday in December

ONE-YEAR BIBLE PLAN: JONAH 1-2 / REV. CHAP. 4&5

NEW CHRISTIANS DISAPPOINTMENTS 3/3

Finally, there is often the problem of:

V. TOO MUCH "NEGATIVE" TEACHING [Disappointed by their preachers].

A. SUCH AS CONSTANTLY EXPOSING DENOMINATIONAL ERRORS: Certainly, there is a place for learning about those in error – **2nd Timothy 4:1-2 AMPC; Acts 20:27.**

But there can be dangers involved in doing so:

#1. If it is done in an arrogant, self-righteous spirit.

#2. If it is done to make us feel good or superior.

#3. If it is done to exclude learning what we need to do.

#4. If we are not careful, it can create carnal Christians, given to strife and envy.

B. WHEN "NEGATIVE" TEACHING IS CALLED FOR: It should be done:

#1. To teach those in error.

#2. Out of love for those in error.

#3. It should be done as Paul did it.

#4. With prayer for their souls - **Romans 10:1.**

#5. With recognition of achievements - **Romans 10:2-4 NIV. #6.** It should be done with the qualities mentioned in **2nd Timothy 2:24-26 AMPC.**

FOUR STAGE OF GROWTH

New Christians may face other disappointments, but I have found these to be quite common.

But it may help to quickly point out that Christians generally go through four stages of spiritual growth:

1. The "ball of fire" stage, following their conversion to Christ.

2. The "reality" stage is when disappointments start.

3. The "up and down" stage: People grow through it to the next stage. Or they fall away or become apathetic **[i.e., "pew-warmers."]**

4. **The steady stage:** Finally, those who persevere reach the stage of **"steady as they go,"** where growth is progressive and steady: *"But the path of the just is like the shining sun, that shines ever brighter unto the perfect day."* **– Proverbs 4:18**

To reach that stage where we will grow steadily, we must have **REALISTIC EXPECTATIONS of future problems.**

We need to be sure we are CONVERTED TO CHRIST, not to the church, a preacher, a teacher, or a friend.

Have YOU been converted to Jesus Christ?

Memory Verse: Proverbs 4:18: *"But the path of the just is like the shining sun, that shines ever brighter unto the perfect day."*

Monday, December 16th

ONE-YEAR BIBLE PLAN: JONAH 3-4 / REV. CHAP. 6&7

Proverbs 19:22-24: *"A man's desire is his kindness: and a poor man is better than a liar. The fear of the LORD tendeth to life: and he that hath it shall abide satisfied......."*

FEAR AND SERVE GOD

Solomon began to desire total satisfaction when he was established as the king of Israel. Enthroned with little or no struggle, Solomon began to live an extravagant lifestyle. He squandered enormous wealth on women and exotic things. At the peak of his reign, he was reputed to be the most famous king in the world, the richest, and the wisest.

Yet, with all his acquisitions and fame, Solomon remained restless and unsatisfied. He had set out to acquire complete satisfaction and peace of mind, yet all his attainments brought him hopelessness and emptiness.

Towards the end of his life, he realized that the search for satisfaction could only be achieved by coming to terms with the creator, Elohim. Solomon surmised, *"Let us hear the conclusion of the whole matter: Fear God, keep His commandments: for this is the whole duty of man."*

King Solomon's conclusion is indeed true. When you fear God, you realize that great opportunities, wonderful relationships, enormous power, high intelligence and ingenuity, great wealth and affluence, health, and beauty are all gifts from God. With such realizations come a better appreciation and, consequently, a better manifestation of God's blessings in your life. *Do you fear and serve God?*

Tuesday, December 17th

ONE-YEAR BIBLE PLAN: MICAH 1-2 / REVELATION 8:1-13

Jeremiah 29:11: *"For I know the plans I have for you,' declares the Lord, 'plans to prosper you and not to harm you, plans to give you hope and a future."*

HIS LEADING

As you start this new day, open your hearts for a timely reminder that God has beautiful plans for your life. In times of uncertainty, this truth will anchor you.

When God first spoke these stirring words through the prophet Jeremiah, the Israelites languished as exiles in Babylon. Every dream for their future seemed shattered. But God had not forgotten them—His perfect plans remained. A future filled with hope awaited.

Just as surely as God held the Israelites in His hands, He holds you and me securely today.

When our limited vision sees only setbacks and heartaches, God sees the unfolding masterpiece of His will on the canvas of our lives.

We may need help to grasp how our current struggles fit into the mosaic of His grand design, but we can surely trust in the One who is making all things beautiful in time.

Prayer:

Father, Teach me to find purpose and peace as I rest in the promise of Your beautiful plans. Attune my heart to the whispered wisdom of Your Spirit in Jesus' Name, Amen.

Wednesday, December 18th

ONE-YEAR BIBLE PLAN: MICAH 3-4 / REVELATION 9:1-21

CHURCH MEMBERSHIP 1/4

People often seek church membership soon after conversion or when moving to a new area. They desire to become members of a local congregation. Which is a good thing for both them and the church. Often, there are questions regarding church membership, such as:

1. What is church membership?
2. Is church membership really necessary?
3. What benefits are there to church membership?
4. What obligations are there to church membership?
5. How does one become a member of the church?

In this study, we seek to answer such questions.

I. THE CHURCH UNIVERSAL DEFINED:

1. The universal church is the church Jesus promised to build in **Matthew 16:18 AMPC.**

2. It is referred to called Christ - **Ephesians 1:22-23.**

3. There is only One Body, or Church - **Ephesians 4:4.**

4. This body comprises individual members - **Romans 12:4-5 NIV; TLB; 1st Corinthians 12:27 AMPC.**

The universal church consists of all Christians, with Christ as the head.

Memory Verse: Matthew 16:18: *"And I also say to you that you are Peter, and on this rock, I will build My church, and the gates of Hades shall not prevail against it."*

Thursday, December 19th

ONE-YEAR BIBLE PLAN: MICAH 5-7 / REVELATION 10:1-11

Proverbs 29:11: *"A fool uttereth all his mind: but a wise man keepeth it in till afterward."*

BE QUIET

Believers must learn to keep their mouths shut. Very few of us have mastered that skill. When we get our backs up about something, we must inform everyone. *"I'm just going to give them a piece of my mind,"* we say. Don't make that mistake. No one wants or needs a piece of your mind—and if you give it to them, you'll only end up alienating people and bringing harm to yourself. Learn, instead, to keep quiet.

This especially applies in the area of spiritual insight. When the Holy Spirit gives you discernment about a situation, don't go spreading it all over town. If you do, you'll come to the place where the Lord can't trust you with revelation and insight into things and situations.

I've seen that happen. I've known intercessors who have received revelations about someone's weaknesses or needs. They have been given insight into the problem in someone's life so that they could pray for that person. But, instead of keeping that information between themselves and God in prayer, they told others about it. As a result, they lost their effectiveness as intercessors.

Don't let that happen to you. Develop the quiet art of the wise man, and the devil will find it increasingly difficult to harm your prayer life and ministry to others.

Prayer: *Lord, give the grace to be quiet in Jesus' Name.*

Friday, December 20th

ONE-YEAR BIBLE PLAN: NAHUM 1-3 / REVELATION 11:1-19

Hebrews 11:1: *"Now faith is the substance of things hoped for, the evidence of things not seen."*

FAITH NOW

So often, we have faith in the future. We believe "one day" God is going to do something great. "One day," we'll get a good break. "One day," we'll feel better. "One day," the problem will turn around. It's good to have faith in the future and believe that God will take care of us, but we can become so future-minded that we lose sight of the fact that God wants to do something great in our lives today.

Today, God wants to show you favor. Today, God wants to amaze you with His goodness. He is called "the Great I Am," not "the Great I Was" or "the Great I Will Be." God is always in the present, and true faith is always in the present.

Faith in the future is good, but you must start releasing your faith for now. The Scripture says, *"Now faith is."* The faith that's alive and active is your faith for today. Every morning, we should get up with the attitude, *"Something good is going to happen to me today!"*

Prayer:

Father, today I ask for a breakthrough. I pray that You will send a favor today. I pray that You will send restoration today. I pray that You will send healing today. Thank You in advance for Your goodness and grace today and every day of my life, in Jesus' Name! Amen.

Saturday, December 21st

ONE-YEAR BIBLE PLAN: HAB. 1-3 / REVELATION 12:1-17

WISDOM OF THE ORACLE

NEWS WITHOUT THE NOISE

- The faithful man is never known by noisemaking but by news making. **Proverbs 20:6; Psalms 12:1.**
- He does not make a proclamation but a demonstration.
- A man is not known by his alone but by his faithfulness works.
- Faithfulness does not speak; it simply shows.
- It is never known to explain but to display.
- It is shy to go to the open but content to serve and contribute secretly.
- Men see in the open and commend such, but God sees in the secret and rewards such.
- Faithfulness values and esteem rewards rather than commendation.

Fourth Sunday in December

ONE-YEAR BIBLE PLAN: ZEPH. 1-3 / REVELATION 13:1-18

CHURCH MEMBERSHIP 2/4

B. PRIVILEGES:

1. Those in this church are saved, as Christ is the Savior of the body - **Ephesians 5:23 TLB; Ephesians 5:22-24 MSG.**

2. They enjoy all spiritual blessings found only in Christ - **Ephesians 1:3 MSG.**

3. Such blessings include forgiveness of sins - **Ephesians 1:7.**

4. Such blessings include the privilege of prayer - **Hebrews 4:14-16 AMPC.**

5. Those in the church universally enjoy blessings now and in the future.

C. OBLIGATIONS:

1. To remain connected to the Head, [Christ] - **John 15:1-8 AMPC.**

2. To do their part in the body - **Ephesians 4:15-16 AMPC, MSG.**

3. To fulfill whatever function they can - **Romans 12:4-8 AMPC.**

4. To love the brotherhood [all Christians] – **1st Peter 2:17 AMPC; 1st Peter 1:22-23 AMPC; 1st Peter 3:8-9.**

Membership has its privileges, but it also has its obligations.

D. BECOMING A MEMBER:

1. Those baptized were "added" - **Acts 2:41.**

2. The Lord added those being saved to His church - **Acts 2:46-47.**

3. By One Spirit, they were baptized into one body [the church] – **1ˢᵗ Corinthians 12:13-14; Titus 3:4-5.**
4. One becomes a member of the church universally when they are saved.
5. If one wishes to be a church member universally, one needs to obey the gospel of Christ in faith, repentance, and baptism. **Mark 16:15-16; Acts 2:38-42.**
6. Then, they are ready to become members.

Memory Verse: Acts 2:41: *"Then those who gladly received his word were baptized, and that day about three thousand souls were added to them."*

Monday, December 23rd

ONE-YEAR BIBLE PLAN: HAGGAI 1-2 / REVELATION 14:1-20

Acts 3:1-11: *".... And they were filled with wonder and amazement at what had happened unto him."*

HOPE

Just imagine the life of the disabled man at the beautiful gate in **Acts 3:1-3**. He was lamed from birth, connoting stagnancy. He did not stand a chance of ever amounting to anything worth writing home about. Every given day, for forty years, he was carried to beg for alms at the gate of the temple called Beautiful. What a life!

But one day, hope came for the hopeless cripple as he encountered the power of the risen Christ, and things instantly changed miraculously in his life. **Acts 3:10** says, *"And they knew that it was he who sat for alms at the Beautiful gate of the temple: and they were filled with wonder and amazement at that which had happened unto him."*

The life of the lame man, which was a reproach and a source of sorrow, pity, and ridicule, was drastically changed into an amazing testimony after connecting to the messenger of Jesus Christ.

Is there any area of your life that is crippled or lamed? Is your business, finances, marriage, career, or health stagnating? What has been a source of pain and concern over the years? Is it failure, disease, sickness, childlessness, loneliness, singleness, bareness, or joblessness? *Whatsoever it may be, today, and as you have hope, and because of the anointing, I charge that lame spirit to depart from you in The Name of Jesus Christ. Amen!*

Tuesday, December 24th

ONE-YEAR BIBLE PLAN: ZECH. 1-2 / REVELATION 15:1-8

Ecclesiastes 3:1: *"There is a time for everything and a season for every activity under the heavens:"*

A NEW SEASON

Today, embrace life's seasons, knowing there is a divine purpose in every time and activity. Remember, with God's grace, there's no season you can't weather. As you step into this new day, carry the wisdom of **Ecclesiastes 3:1** in your hearts. This profound scripture reminds us of the divinely orchestrated rhythm of life, where each moment and activity has a designated time in God's grand design for us.

Life is a beautiful tapestry of seasons - times of joy and sorrow, growth and rest, silence and celebration. Each season has its purpose and its lessons. In seasons of joy and prosperity, we are reminded of God's abundant blessings and the joy of living in His grace. In seasons of adversity and sorrow, we can lean into God's unfailing strength and experience His comfort more deeply.

In every season, God is with us, guiding and shaping us. Even when we can't see the purpose of our season, we can trust that God is at work, using each moment to mold us into the people He wants us to be.

So today, ask yourself: What season am I in right now? How is God using this season to shape me? Can I trust God's timing and purpose, even if I don't understand it?

Prayer: *Lord, in this season, mold me into what You designed me to be in Jesus' Name. Amen!*

Wednesday, December 25th

ONE-YEAR BIBLE PLAN: ZECH. 3-4 / REVELATION 16:1-21

CHURCH MEMBERSHIP 3/4

II. IN THE CHURCH LOCAL

A. DEFINITION: The local church is a group of Christians who meet and work together – **1st Thessalonians 1:1.**

There are many such churches, not just one - **Romans 16:1 MSG; Galatians 1:2 TLB; Acts 9:31.**

Some form of membership in such churches is indicated - e.g., **Romans 16:1 TLB; Romans 16:5.**

The local church comprises Christians who agree to work together in one location.

B. PRIVILEGES:

1. A spiritual family **Mark 10:28-31; 1st Timothy 5:1-2.**
2. Strength from older Christians – **Romans 15:1 AMPC; Galatians 6:1 MSG.**
3. Mutual comfort in addition to that received from God – **2nd Corinthians 1:3-5 AMPC.**
4. **The prayers of brethren – James 5:14-16 AMPC.**
5. Those in local churches enjoy blessings not experienced by "floaters."

> **Memory Verse: Galatians 6:1:** *"Brethren, if a man is overtaken in any trespass, you who are spiritual restore such a one in a spirit of gentleness, considering yourself lest you also be tempted."*

Thursday, December 26th

ONE-YEAR BIBLE PLAN: ZECH. 5-6/ REVELATION 17:1-18

Romans 5:2 TPT: *"Our faith guarantees us permanent access to this marvelous kindness that has given us a perfect relationship with God. What incredible joy bursts within us as we celebrate our hope of experiencing God's glory!"*

REJOICE IN HOPE

Are you sick in your body? Are you stranded? Are you financially frustrated? In every area of your life that you have a need, all is well. Why? We are standing by faith in the place of grace. We are standing on a favored ground. In other words, your ground will always produce. You stand on favored ground, and nothing works against you.

As a result of our standing, we are celebrating and rejoicing in hope. Hope means a joyful, confident expectation that things will turn out well. So, we now have peace with God and stand on the favored ground.

All is now well with the believer, and nothing works against you. No challenge, no difficulty, and no circumstance work against you. All things are working together for your good. God is putting the pieces and the puzzles together in your favor.

And it is because of the death, burial, and resurrection of Jesus Christ. In **John 19:30**, Jesus said: *"It is finished."* It is finished was the master stroke against the powers of hell. The devil had no answer to that statement. Therefore, no matter what you are going through, there is hope. It is not over yet. It will turn out for your good, so rejoice in hope.

Friday, December 27th

ONE-YEAR BIBLE PLAN: ZECH. 7-8 / REVELATION 18:1-24

John 16:21-24: *"A woman, when she is in labor, has sorrow because her hour has come; but as soon as she has given birth to the child, she no longer remembers the anguish, for joy that a human being has been born into the world...."*

YOUR JOY

In today's passage, Jesus Christ prepared to leave His disciples, bringing sorrow to their hearts. He used the scenario of a woman in the travail of childbirth one moment and rejoicing the next to assure them that their sorrow would eventually turn to joy.

The joy that would come to the disciples would cancel their sorrow. He told them, *"And ye therefore now have sorrow, but I will see you again, and your heart shall rejoice, and your joy no man takes from you."* **John 16:22** agrees with the Psalmist's declaration that *"weeping may endure for a night, but joy comes in the morning."* **Psalm 30:5.**

Beloved, your season of joy is very close. It does not matter what you are going through now; God promises you will exchange your sorrow for joy.

Your suffering can be a result of satanic affliction, hatred from family and friends, or a test of faith. It could also be based on your faith. Your Christian position on issues of life could also land you in the wilderness of pain or sorrow. *The heart-warming promise of the Lord is that your sorrow shall turn to joy, and no one will take your joy from you in the Name of Jesus Christ. Amen!*

Saturday, December 28th

ONE-YEAR BIBLE PLAN: ZECH. 9-11 / REVELATION

WISDOM OF THE ORACLE

HEART BEFORE ACT

- o Serving God heartily and actively are both required for rewardable services, but hearty service is more fundamental.

- o God sees the state of the heart, but men notice the act.

- o Our heart reaches Him before our acts.

- o Men may commend your acts visible to all, but only God can commend your heart because only Him can access them. **1ST Samuel 16:7; 2nd Chronicles 16:9; Jeremiah 17:9-10.**

Fifth Sunday, December 29th

ONE-YEAR BIBLE PLAN: ZECH. 12-14/ REVELATION 20:1-15

CHURCH MEMBERSHIP 4/4

IN THE CHURCH, LOCAL

C. OBLIGATIONS:

1. To bear one another's burdens **Galatians 6:2 AMPC.**

2. To encourage one another - **Hebrews 3:12-14.**

3. To assemble - **Hebrews 10:24-25; Acts 20:7.**

4. To serve one another with whatever abilities we have – **1st Peter 4:10-11.**

5. To care for one another, and to seek peace – **1st Thessalonians 5:11-15.**

6. To withdraw from brethren walking disorderly – **2nd Thessalonians 3:6-15.**

7. Membership has its privileges, but it also has its obligations.

D. BECOMING A MEMBER:

1. Membership in a local congregation is not automatic, e.g., the eunuch - **Acts 8:39**

2. It must be sought out by an individual, e.g., Saul - **Acts 9:26a**

3. The congregation must be willing to extend fellowship, e.g., Jerusalem - **Acts 9:26b.**

4. A recommendation can help expedite the process, e.g., Barnabas - **Acts 9:27-28.**

VETTING

The actual vetting process may vary from congregation to congregation.

1. A person becomes a member of a local church when they are accepted as such.

2. Church membership is a worthy aspiration.

Membership in the church universal is necessary for salvation.

Membership in the local church is needed for spiritual growth and service.

Church membership in both aspects is attained: First, we are added to the church universal by the Lord when we are saved, then when we join ourselves to a local church through mutual consent to work together.

Have you become a universal church member through obeying the gospel of Christ?

Have you become a local church member to fulfill your duties to Christ and His brethren?

Memory Verse: 1st Peter 4:10-11: *"As each one has received a gift, minister it to one another, as good stewards of the manifold grace of God. 11 If anyone speaks, let him speak as the oracles of God. If anyone ministers, let him do it as with the ability which God supplies, that in all things God may be glorified through Jesus Christ, to whom belong the glory and the dominion forever and ever. Amen."*

Monday, December 30th

ONE-YEAR BIBLE PLAN: MALACHI 1-2 / REVELATION 21:1-27

Esther 5:1-3: *".... she obtained favor in his sight: and the king held out to Esther the golden scepter in his hand...."*

DIVINE ARRANGEMENT

These days, there are no kings with the kind of power and authority wielded by King Ahasuerus. Whereas democracies and weak monarchies derive power from the people they govern, the kings of old were absolute monarchs, demi-gods whose words or even body movements were laws. Ahasuerus was one of such kings. He was an extreme dictator who could convict or pardon a person by mere movement of his wand.

History remembers him as a highly impulsive king who once ordered the sea to be punished with three hundred strokes of whips for disobeying him in allowing the bridge he built over the sea to collapse. His high level of emotional instability was legendary. In those days, within the length and breadth of the kingdom of Persia and Media, going against his command was tantamount to suicide.

So, when Esther appeared before him uninvited, the odds were against her. She would be put to death according to the law of the land, except the King raised his wand to admit her. Going by his antecedents, one would not have expected Esther to live beyond that day. But according to God's divine arrangement, not only was Esther admitted by the king, but also the king promised to fulfill unto her whatever she requested. Surely, such favor is uncommon. *Such is yours today, in Jesus' Name. Amen!*

Tuesday, December 31st

ONE-YEAR BIBLE PLAN: MALACHI 3-4 / REVELATION 22:1-21

Ecclesiastes 3:1: *"To everything there is a season, and a time to every purpose under the heaven:"*

MY SEASON OF CELEBRATING HAS COME!

Isaiah 48:21; Psalm 23:6:

As I continue to follow God's leading, only goodness, mercy, and favor will follow me all through 2025 in Jesus' Name!

Psalm 126:1-6; 1st Corinthians 2:9:

Through my undying love for God, the kind of turnaround that I have never imagined would begin in my life this year!

Psalm 91:1-16:

As I continue to dwell in the secret place of the Most High, I will be exempted from all evils in 2025 and beyond!

Psalm 30:5:

As I continue promoting the kingdom of God through prayers, all my secret tears will be turned into public testimonies in the New Year!

Job 36:11/ Psalm 35:27:

As I continue to serve God diligently, I will spend my days in prosperity and my years in pleasure!

www.ingramcontent.com/pod-product-compliance
Lightning Source LLC
LaVergne TN
LVHW021811060526
838201LV00058B/3334